Career Puzzle

6 Interlocking Pieces
to Land a Job You'll Love
and Get Paid What You're Worth

Donald Reinsel

Copyright © 2014 Donald Reinsel

All Rights Reserved

Year of the Book
Glen Rock, PA
yotbpress.com

ISBN 13: 978-0-9912716-2-7
ISBN 10: 0-9912716-2-9

Library of Congress Control Number: 2014939181

Dedication

To Stacy
For the time and freedom I was given in pursuit of this endeavor

Table of Contents

Introduction i

Chapter 1 - Your Resume 1
    The Tools 2
    The Rules 6
    The Recommendations 8
    The Parts 11
    The Review 30
    Distribution Methods 31
    Examples 32

Chapter 2 – Your Portfolio 37
    What Is It? 37
    Why Have One? 37
    Where Should I Start? 38
    What Should Be Included? 38
    What Shouldn't Be Included? 38
    How Should It Be Organized? 39
    What Medium Should I Use? 41
    What Materials Are Needed? 44
    What Are My Resources? 63
    How Do I Use My Portfolio? 64
    Should I Add To My Portfolio? 66

Chapter 3 – Your Education 69
- Formal Learning 70
- Informal Learning 81

Chapter 4 – Your Personal Finances 91
- What is Personal Finance? 92
- Why Credit Matters 93
- Financing - What Do Things Really Cost? 95
- What Is Your Credit Score? 98
- The Costs of Living 100
- Organizing and Tracking Your Finances 125
- Paying it Down and Saving it Up 129

Chapter 5 – Communication 133
- Formal Communication 134
- Informal Communication 182

Chapter 6 - Marketing & Selling Yourself 187
- Marketing - Generating Interest 188
- Managing the Process - *The Sales Pipeline* 217
- Selling - Closing the Deal 230

The Wrap-up 237

About the Author 239

Introduction

If you are not paying attention, half a million dollars or more can easily slip through your fingers over the life of your career. Salary, raises, promotions, bonuses, and other benefits are just some of the ways it happens. Over time, missed opportunities, due to a lack of preparation, can become detrimental to your career and greatly decrease your earning potential. If you don't want this to happen, you'll need to learn the rules of the game, start thinking of yourself as a business, and act accordingly. In the chapters that follow, we look at best practices followed by successful businesses to help you establish a framework for success.

Successful businesses sell products and/or services at a profit. If you think about it, you have to do the same thing by working (offering your skills and expertise) in exchange for payment (hourly wage or salary). That's only half the story. You also have to take care of the bottom line. That means, generating enough income to cover the cost of life's necessities (food, clothing, shelter, etc.). The more adept you are at running your business, the better the chance you have of achieving all the possibilities that life has to offer.

This book focuses on those areas that help you operate in a way that maximizes your earning potential. To help you accomplish this, we look at the basic fundamentals necessary to the survival and success of any business or individual. These broad themes include communication, finance, and education. We further break this down into six specific areas that will have the greatest impact on your career and life. As you read this book, we recommend implementing the suggestions from each chapter. Let this be a starting point in your quest for more knowledge. Your life will be better off for it.

Chapter 1 - Your Resume

"Always be a first-rate version of yourself, instead of a second-rate version of somebody else." - Judy Garland -

Your resume is a ticket to the most important single-elimination tournament on the planet. If you win, you get to move to the next round of the hiring process with your hopes of landing that dream job. If you lose, you go home. This book is devoted to helping you win each round of the hiring process and getting the job you want. To get past the first round however, you'll need to construct a resume that is so compelling anyone coming in contact with it wants to pick it up and read it.

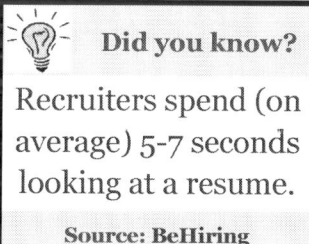

A captivating resume does three things well. First, it must attract attention by being visually pleasing. Resumes that are formatted correctly get attention over those that aren't. Looks count in life and resumes are no different. Second, it must be persuasive enough to keep the reader's attention. Your resume must be worded in just the right way to convince the reader you are the best person for the job. Finally, your resume must motivate the reader to take action. That means contacting you so they can learn more about you. If your resume does these three things, you'll be well on your way to winning the first round.

While this chapter focuses exclusively on helping you build a great resume, you'll also find it:

- ➢ Provides you with the confidence, talking points, and focus needed throughout your job search.
- ➢ Properly organizes your experiences into a compelling document that describes you like no one else can.
- ➢ Allows you to be ready for opportunities that happen quickly and just as quickly go away.

To make this process as easy and straightforward as possible, we have divided the chapter into seven sections: Tools, Rules, Recommendations, Parts, Review, Distribution, and Examples. We suggest reading the entire chapter first to get an idea of how all the pieces fit together. Once you have everything in place to start writing, go back to Step 4 "Parts." This section provides the necessary step-by-step instructions needed to help you write a winning resume.

Great things are often accomplished in small steps and your resume is no exception. Build it one piece at a time using the recommendations listed below. Don't be tempted to move to the next section until you are happy with what you have written. Read a section, write a part. Repeating this process and using the suggestions in this chapter will help you build a great resume. Great resumes get you noticed, get you interviews, and most importantly get you job offers. Are you ready to win the first round?

The Tools

Before starting this or any endeavor, it is important to have the proper tools and resources available in order to maximize your opportunities for success. With that in mind, we recommend you have access to the following:

Computer and printer

If you don't own a computer and printer, check the availability at your school, local library, or career center.

Software program

Know or become familiar with a word processing program. The most common and widely used is Microsoft Word. However, there are many other programs like WordPerfect, TextMaker, and Apple Pages that can do the job just as well. Regardless of which one you use, make sure you know enough about the basics to construct a great looking resume. Need some help? Ask friends and family, take a class, or watch one of the many tutorials available on YouTube www.youtube.com.

Documentation

Before you begin typing your resume, gather any supporting documents that help confirm your experiences relating to work, education, and other activities. Items like transcripts, job descriptions, dates worked, along with any honors or awards will help you complete your resume faster and lessen the chance of errors.

Storage/Backups

As your resume begins to take shape, make sure your time and effort is protected by periodically saving your work. Below we list some ways in which you can store and easily retrieve your information:

Locally

> - Create a folder on your computer. Make it easy to find by putting it on your computer's desktop. In Figure 1.1, the file folder is easy to locate in the lower right corner. This is often the first screen you'll see when your computer starts up and makes accessing your resume very easy.

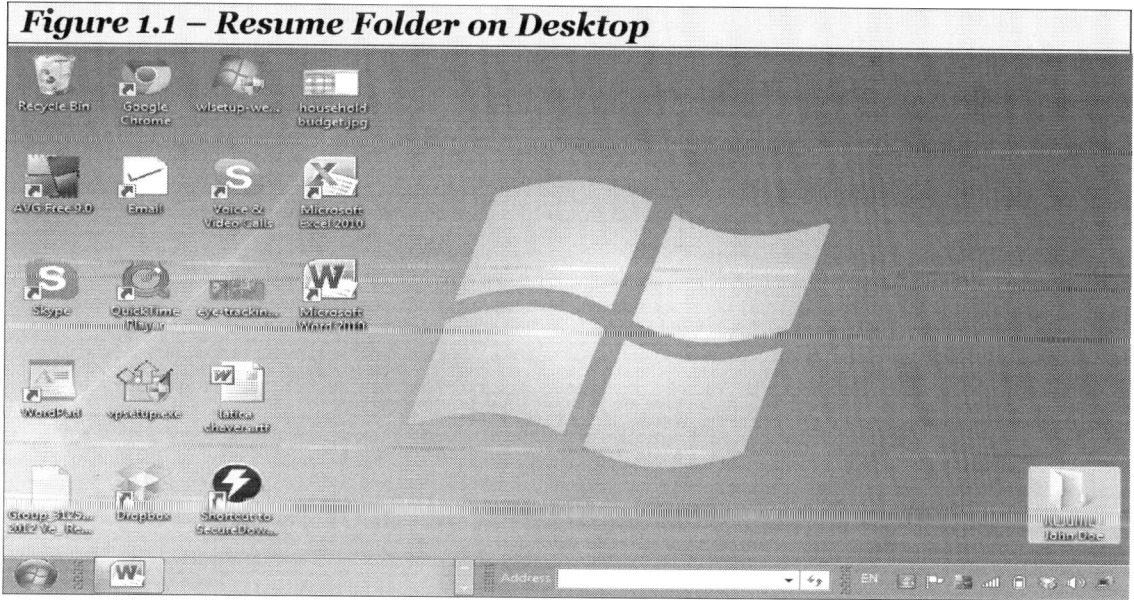

Figure 1.1 – Resume Folder on Desktop

Your Resume

Figure 1.2 – Resume Folder Creation

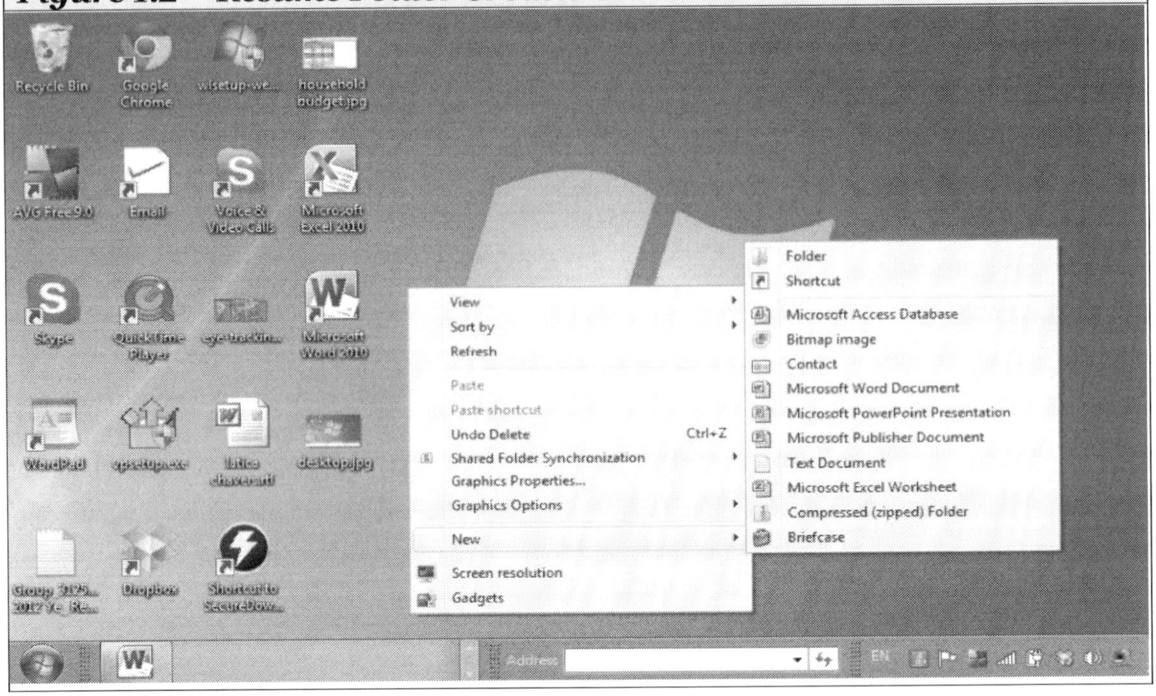

To make a folder like the one shown in Figure 1.1, go to the desktop screen and right click on your mouse. This will open up a menu. Scroll down and choose new. This will open up a second menu. Choose the first item (folder) on the second menu as shown in Figure 1.2 above and give it a name.

When naming the folder, use a descriptive title to avoid any confusion. A good way to do this is by describing what the folder contains and who it is for. In Figure 1.1, we named our folder Resume – John Doe.

> If you don't own a computer and have to use one in a public place such as a library, school, or career center, save your work to a portable flash drive like the one shown in Figure 1.3.

Figure 1.3 Storage Device

Ideally, you'll want to save your work in at least two different locations to guard against loss. Saving a copy on your computer and a flash drive, as noted above, is a viable solution. However, you may want to consider using The Cloud as a way to store and easily access your information.

The Cloud

Instead of trying to keep track of which device (PC, laptop, tablet, etc.) your resume is located on, why not put it in The Cloud? The Cloud allows you to work, store and access your resume without having to save it to your computer's hard drive or a portable flash drive. Getting your information to the cloud can be accomplished by:

- ➢ Using a program like Microsoft Word, or one of the many others mentioned above, to type your resume and upload it to a cloud-based service like Dropbox www.dropbox.net, FileSwap www.fileswap.com, and many other similar companies.

- ➢ Using a free cloud-based word processing program like Google Docs, Zoho Docs http://www.zoho.com/docs/, ThinkFree http://www.thinkfree.com/main.jsp and Microsoft's OneDrive https://onedrive.live.com/about/en-us.

- ➢ Of this group, Google Docs http://docs.google.com, is probably the most popular and widely used. It also allows you to create a variety of different files (documents, spreadsheets, presentations, etc.). However, they often lack features of other popular software programs (Word, WordPerfect, Apple Pages, etc.).

The main benefit of The Cloud is having universal access to your documents. A computer with an internet connection is all that is needed to retrieve your work from anywhere.

Paper

Technology has greatly diminished the need for printing and mailing resumes. However, you will still need a printed copy because:

- ➢ The interviewer may not have your resume for some reason. Providing them with a copy makes you look prepared and organized.

- ➢ You may interview with several people and they in turn may not have your resume.

> The contents of your resume may have changed due to a lengthy interval between the application and interview process. If this is the case, retrieve the version of your resume submitted in the initial application process. Follow the recommendations outlined in Chapter 6 (Managing the Process – The Sales Pipeline) to make this process as smooth as possible.

Having the correct resume version at an interview is critical to your success. If you have an updated version that differs from your initial application, bring it along and highlight any new accomplishments, skills, awards, certifications, etc.

Finally, don't cut corners when it comes to printing your resume. Buy a package of good quality white paper from an office supply store to complement all your hard work.

Support

Leave nothing to chance by making sure you have someone available to review and critique your resume for grammar, punctuation, and form. It is critical to have at least one other pair of eyes taking a constructive look at your work.

The Rules

Originality

Your life experiences are unique! It's up to you to convince prospective employers why you are exceptional and the best candidate for the job. The only way to make that happen is by writing <u>your</u> resume in <u>your</u> words. You are the most capable and best person to describe you. It's okay to get help and ideas from other people, but ultimately the words and ideas you put on paper must be your own. It's important because the work you put in now will help you in later stages of the job search.

Honesty

Did you know?
53% of resumes and job applications contain falsifications.
www.statisticbrain.com

Competition for jobs remains fierce with approximately three unemployed people vying for every job opening according to a recent Bureau of Labor Statistics survey. Because the stakes are so high, many job seekers will do anything to gain a competitive edge. Unfortunately, this means many applicants will misrepresent their credentials to increase the chances of success. While it may seem tempting, don't falsify, distort, or exaggerate your qualifications. Be as honest as possible. Technology has made it easier than ever for employers to check your background and credentials.

Errors

Errors are an issue of trust. The resume is the first project you will complete for a company. Therefore, it has to be perfect and not contain spelling or grammatical errors. If it does, that trust is irrevocably broken and your chances of getting hired are almost zero. How can you make sure it's error free?

- Allow for a certain amount of time between the creation and proofreading of your resume. This break will give you a fresh perspective when it's time to continue your work.

- Have others read your resume for grammar and spelling accuracy like:
    - Friends and Family
    - School Guidance Counselors
    - College - Career Services
    - Professional Resume Writers and Reviewers (Available locally and on the Internet)

- Proofread with a twist. Start at the bottom of your resume and read everything in reverse. This does not let your mind assume correctness when read normally.

Length

Your resume is a story about you and will vary from everyone else's in content, style, and length. If you are new to the job market and seek an entry level position, your story will probably not fill up more than one page. If you have several years of work experience, with a broad range of knowledge, you'll likely have a longer story to tell that may take more than one page. Regardless of how long it takes to tell your story, make each word count. If that means your resume needs to be two or more pages, go for it as one size does not fit all. Just be aware employers want short, concise writing that gets to the point. A longer resume may be an indicator of your inability to synthesize information into short and succinct thoughts, a skill that is increasingly valued in today's world of information overload.

Similarities

Per www.smarterer.com, "Make sure your Facebook, Twitter, LinkedIn and any other public profiles *are professional* and don't contradict the information contained in your resume. You're an impressive candidate, and your on-line presence should enhance, not destroy, that image."

The Recommendations

Appearance

Looks matter and your resume is no exception. This seems to confirm a recent study by The Ladders http://www.theladders.com/ that noted, "On average, recruiters spent six seconds to make the initial decision on whether to trash your resume or consider you for the position." The study also found, "visual features such as pictures, graphs, and ads (on employment-related sites like LinkedIn) are distracting, eating up precious time and reducing the recruiter's decision-making ability."

This underscores the importance of a properly formatted resume. Those that look and feel professional will get more attention than their poorly constructed counterparts. Given that only a short amount of time may be allotted to your resume, it must immediately captivate the reader's attention by being properly balanced.

That consists of what is (content) and is not (white space) on your resume as noted below.

Content

Use suitable margins with consistent fonts and sizes throughout. Feel free to use different typefaces (bold, *italic*) where needed, but don't overdo it, especially with the use of bullet points. Make it easy for the reader to get to know you. What parts of your resume does the reader focus on? According to The Ladders, "Recruiters spend nearly 80% of their time focusing on six different areas of a resume." The most-important ones are:

- Your name
- Current title/company
- Previous title/company
- Current position start and end dates
- Previous position start and end dates
- Education

Make sure these items are accurate and placed correctly on your resume.

White Space

Are there blank areas on your resume? To be pleasing to the eye, your resume must be a proper balance of white space and words. There can be a tendency to cram as much as possible onto one page even if it means using a smaller than normal font. This approach can leave your resume looking crowded, cluttered, and hard to read. Less is better. If extra room is needed, use a second or third page or incorporate some of the key points from your resume into your cover letter or application.

Job Duties vs. Achievements

This is one of the most important sections of your resume and will probably require most of your time. It can be very easy to fall into the trap of just listing the duties of your current and past jobs. Will that really captivate someone's interest and separate you from your competition? Will it tell your story in the most fascinating way possible? Probably not! Instead, highlight your achievements by describing how your contributions made a difference in the success of the company. Did you:

- Save the company money?
- Find a way to save time and do things differently?
- Help the organization become more streamlined?
- Help the company become more profitable?

Examine your past and present jobs with these types of questions in mind along with any others you can think of. Your answers will allow you to tell the most compelling story possible and make the reader want to hear more.

Relevancy

Rarely, if ever, will your qualifications exactly match the job description. Therefore, you may need to make changes to your resume so it is in alignment with the duties of the job listing. To make your resume and job description more compatible, read over the job description at least twice. Now, look at your resume. Does it include some of the same key words or phrases used in the job description? If not, incorporate some of those expressions into your resume. This is becoming more important as companies are increasingly relying on technology to scan resumes and applications for key words and phrases.

It's okay to have a basic template for your resume and cover letter but be prepared to alter them for every job you apply to. In Chapter 5, we show you how to make your resume, cover letter, and job description work together. To get that process started, follow the recommended steps listed in the Parts section of this chapter. When finished, you'll have a completed resume that is ready to use in your job search.

Applicability

Do your skills, experience, and education match up with the jobs you are applying for? If not, you may be wasting valuable time. Increase your chances of success by only applying to those positions in which you have at least 80% of the qualifications listed.

Cover letter

Always include a cover letter when applying for a job. The resume and cover letter are traveling partners that complement each other. What you sacrifice in keeping your resume brief and to the point, can be more thoroughly explained in the cover letter. It is often the best way to:

- Describe why your skill sets match the needs of the advertised position.
- Explain any gaps in employment or other extenuating circumstances.
- Expand on any questions your resume fails to answer.

The Parts

While your resume will differ in appearance and content from your competition, it still must contain certain elements common to all candidates. We now discuss each part of the resume using a step-by-step approach. We encourage you to construct your resume as you read along with this section of the book.

Step 1: Contact Information

Think of your resume as a very small but valuable piece of real estate. Accordingly, every part plays an extremely important role due to the limited availability of space. Your contact information is no exception and is one of the areas recruiters focus on when scanning resumes as noted above.

Because this section often receives a great deal of scrutiny, it is very important it be as up-to-date and accurate as possible. If your contact information is wrong or too hard for a prospective employer to reach you, they will likely move on to the next suitable candidate. Therefore, be sure to include your full name, permanent and local addresses, phone number (including area code), a professional sounding email address, and web page (if applicable) as shown in Figure 1.4 below.

Figure 1.4 - Resume Heading

Jane J. Jobseeker
123 Main Street
Anywhereville, PA 12345
(123) 456-7890
<u>jane.jobseeker@email.com</u>

Your contact information needs to stand out from the rest of the resume. Use a larger font size and separate it from the rest of the resume by a solid horizontal line. Your name should stand out even more by being bolder and larger than the rest of the text in this section. For the example above, we used a font size of 18 and bolded the name **Jane J. Jobseeker**. The remaining lines use a smaller font size of 14, but are still larger than the font size of eleven used for the text of the resume. Also, if your resume is longer than one page, repeat your heading exactly the same way on subsequent pages.

Step 2: Professional/Work Experience

Work experiences, including paid and unpaid internships, should be listed starting with the most recent. For each experience, list the company name, location (city and state), dates of employment, and your job title(s). Underneath this information, list your achievements and accomplishments. As noted previously, ***don't fall into the trap of listing just your duties and responsibilities.*** This is a story about you, your efforts, and how they impacted each company you have worked for. Make it interesting by using action words that more fully describe your accomplishments and how they benefit(ed) the company. Figures 1.5 and 1.6 highlight the differences of these two approaches.

Figure 1.5 - Professional Experience (Duties and Responsibilities)

Administrative Assistant   **2010 - Present**
Acme Company
Anywhereville, PA

- Answer telephone and forward calls to the appropriate person
- Type and distribute memorandums
- Distribute incoming mail to employee inboxes and deliver mail to post office
- Make travel and meeting room accommodations for senior staff
- Help marketing department on an as needed basis

Figure 1.6 - Professional Experience (Accomplishments & Achievements)

Administrative Assistant   **2010 - Present**
Acme Company
Anywhereville, PA

- Provide incoming call support for a 25 person company by fully utilizing all features of the company communication network. Continually document and train all staff to ensure consistency and integrity regarding all client interactions

- Compose, review, and distribute all inter-company memorandums

- Researched and implemented more cost effective ways to utilize various mail services resulting in an average cost savings of $65 per month

- Negotiated with a third party vendor to handle all arrangements regarding company travel, accommodations, and meeting rooms resulting in a monthly savings of $450

- Provide project support for the marketing department by assembling advertising packets while adhering to current company protocols to ensure consistency

Notice the difference in the above examples? Figure 1.5 lists just the duties and responsibilities performed by our fictional candidate Jane J. Jobseeker. While it may succinctly describe what she does, it is uninspiring to the reader and does nothing to differentiate her from the other candidates.

The second approach, Figure 1.6, shows how the employee's actions positively benefit the company. What makes a greater impact, just listing duties and responsibilities or highlighting accomplishments and achievements? Make the choice easy for your future employer to pick you. Show them how you are different from other candidates and how your past accomplishments and achievements translate to future performance.

Going forward, just don't do a job, own it! Embrace it and learn every aspect of your job, your co-workers' jobs and as many other people as possible. This will:

- Make you a valued team member with greater job security.
- Increase your worth by learning new skill sets.
- Help you see the big picture (conceptual skills) and how you and everyone else's jobs fits together.
- Allow you to more easily write a resume that lists accomplishments and achievements rather than just duties and responsibilities.

If you are writing your resume, as you read this book, you should now have two sections completed (the heading and your work experiences) as shown in Figure 1.7.

Figure 1.7 - Heading + Professional Experience

Jane J. Jobseeker

123 Main Street
Anywhereville, PA 12345
(123) 456-7890
jane.jobseeker@email.com

Professional Experience

Administrative Assistant   2010 - Present
Acme Company
Anywhereville, PA

- Provide incoming call support for a 25 person company by fully utilizing all features of company communication network. Continually document and train all staff on the communication network to ensure consistency and integrity regarding all client interactions

- Compose, review, and distribute all inter-company memorandums

- Researched and implemented more cost effective ways to utilize various mail services resulting in an average cost savings of $65 per month

- Negotiated with a third party vendor to handle all arrangements regarding company travel, accommodations, and meeting rooms resulting in a monthly savings of $450

- Provide project support for the marketing department by assembling advertising packets and adhering to current company protocols and ensuring consistency

You are now two-thirds of the way to completing the first draft of your resume. Next we turn our attention to education.

Step 3:   Education

List all the schools you attended starting with the most recent. When writing this portion of your resume, keeping the following in mind:

- List the school(s), dates attended, graduation dates, if applicable, certificates, majors and/or minors and any course concentrations.
- If you have graduated from college and have more than three years of work experience, you do not need to list your high school.
- Including your Grade Point Average (GPA) is optional and largely depends upon the following:
  - ❖ Graduation Date. If it has been several years since graduating from high school or college, your GPA may no longer be relevant and does not need to be listed on your resume.
  - ❖ Grade Point Average. If it is above average, 3.0 or higher on a 4.0 scale, you may want to include it. If it is exceptional, 3.5 and above, definitely include on your resume. Regardless, make sure you show how it is calculated. For example 3.6/4.0.
- If you are a recent graduate, list internships, coursework, workshops, and anything else that may enhance your credibility.

Note: This area of your resume should follow the professional experience section. However, if you are still in school, a recent graduate, or if your degree is highly relevant to the job you are seeking, place this information right after the heading.

Figure 1.8 shows a recent graduate with a two-year degree and no employment experience. High school information was included to show a clear timeline of accomplishments since graduation.

Figure 1.8 - Education

CBA Community College, Kroy, PA www.cba.edu
Associate Degree/Computerized Accounting Management May 2013
GPA 3.7/4.0

Relevant Courses:

- Principles of Accounting I, II, III, IV, V, VI
- Income Tax Preparation I, II
- Payroll Preparation
- Principles of Cost Accounting
- Accounting Information Systems I, II

Western Prep High School, Clarion, PA www.wcstprep.edu
College Preparatory June 2011

That's it! Only three sections are needed to complete your resume. To summarize, they are:

> ***Heading/Contact Information*** - Tells the reader who you are, where you live, and how to contact you.

> ***Professional Work/Experience*** – Lets the reader know the extent of your work experiences. This is where you can really shine by highlighting key employment experiences and skill sets.

> ***Education*** - Tells the reader your level of schooling, your major area(s) of study, when and where it took place, and any relevant course work.

In Figure 1.9 below, we put the three elements discussed above together to form a complete resume.

Figure 1.9 - *Heading + Professional Experience + Education*

Jane J. Jobseeker

123 Main Street
Anywhereville, PA 12345
(123) 456-7890
jane.jobseeker@email.com

Professional Experience

Administrative Assistant　　　　　　　　　　　　　　**2010 - Present**
Acme Company　　　　　　　　　　　　　　　　　　www.acmecompany.com
Anywhereville, PA 12346

- Provide incoming call support for a 25 person company by fully utilizing all features of company communication network. Continually document and train all staff on the communication network to ensure consistency and integrity regarding all client interactions

- Compose, review and distribute all inter-company memorandums

- Researched and implemented more cost effective ways to utilize various mail services resulting in an average cost savings of $65 per month

- Negotiated with a third party vendor to handle all arrangements regarding company travel, accommodations, and meeting rooms resulting in a monthly savings of $450

- Provide project support for the marketing department by assembling advertising packets and adhering to current company protocols and ensuring consistency

Education

Western Prep High School, Clarion, PA　　　　　　　www.westprep.edu
College Preparatory　　　　　　　　　　　　　　　　　　*June 2010*

Figure 1.9 above shows a high school graduate with several years of work experience. In figure 1.10, we show what our candidate's resume would look like with a 2-year college degree but with no paid work experience.

Figure 1.10 - College Graduate Without Paid Work Experience

Jane J. Jobseeker

123 Main Street
Anywhereville, PA 12345
(123) 456-7890
jane.jobseeker@email.com

Education

CBA Community College, Kroy, PA — www.cba.edu
Associate Degree/Computerized Accounting Management — May 2013
GPA 3.7/4.0

Relevant Courses:

- Principles of Accounting I, II, III, IV, V, VI
- Income Tax Preparation I, II
- Payroll Preparation
- Principles of Cost Accounting
- Accounting Information Systems I, II

Western Prep High School, Clarion, PA — www.westprep.edu
College Preparatory — June 2011

Professional/Work Experience

Administrative Assistant (Six-Week Internship) — April 2013 - May 2013
ABC Accounting — www.abcaccounting.com
Anytown, PA 12345

- Entered, organized, and reviewed data utilized in supervisor's reports
- Assisted in the preparation of financial statements and other related reports
- Performed a variety of administrative duties, including research, fact checking and organizing client files
- Assisted in the reconciliation of accounts receivable/payable and bank statements
- Worked with the finance team on yearly forecasting efforts

Your Resume

To get a better idea of how resumes can vary, we show our same candidate, Jane J. Jobseeker, as a recent college graduate with several years of prior professional experience in Figure 1.11. Because she is a recent graduate focusing on a new career, we list her education right after the heading but before her professional experience. Her new degree also makes listing her high school graduation less relevant and therefore it was removed.

Figure 1.11 – College Graduate With Paid Work Experience

Jane J. Jobseeker
123 Main Street
Anywhereville, PA 12345
(123) 456-7890
jane.jobseeker@email.com

Education

CBA Community College, Kroy, PA — www.cba.edu
Associate Degree/Computerized Accounting Management — May 2013
GPA 3.7/4.0

Relevant Courses:
- Principles of Accounting I, II, III, IV, V, VI
- Income Tax Preparation I, II
- Payroll Preparation
- Principles of Cost Accounting
- Accounting Information Systems I, II

Professional/Work Experience

Administrative Assistant (Six-Week Internship) — April 2013 - May 2013
ABC Accounting — www.abcaccounting.com
Anytown, PA 12345

- Entered, organized and reviewed data utilized in supervisor's reports
- Assisted in the preparation of financial statements and other related reports
- Performed a variety of administrative duties, including research, fact checking and organizing client files
- Assisted in the reconciliation of accounts receivable/payable and bank statements
- Worked with the finance team on yearly forecasting efforts

Executive Assistant — May 2008 – April 2011
ABC Worldwide — www.abcworldwide.com
Anytown, PA 12347

- Provided a multi-faceted approach in coordinating, organizing, and documenting inter-departmental communication by fully utilizing the company's intranet software
- Enhanced communication between departments and executive team, fostering a sense of teamwork and collaboration
- Negotiated favorable terms and pricing agreements with resorts, vendors, caterers and other providers for service at special events, saving at least $15k annually
- Improved office efficiency by implementing color-coded filing system and introducing additional time-saving measures
- Planned and coordinated PR initiatives, business development events, partner retreats, holiday parties and more

Customer Care Associate — April 2006 - May 2008
Acme Car Rental (Part-time) — www.acmecars.com
Somewhereville, PA 98765

- Professionally detailed interior and exterior of rental cars
- Retrieved and delivered rental cars to various locations
- Trained employees on servicing requirements of all returned vehicles
- Frequently provided procedural suggestions that enhanced service and resulted in higher profitability

Your Resume

Congratulations! If you have been completing your resume as you follow along with this book, you are technically finished. Finished, in the sense that all the elements discussed above have been included. At this point, we encourage you to take a good long look at your resume to make sure you have not forgotten anything. Next, we suggest reading steps four through seven and add any items that will help to better tell your story.

Step 4: Objective

Should I or not? If I do, what should I say? This is a quandary for many on the merits of including, or not including, an objective statement on their resume. There are really two issues concerning the objective statement. First, should it be included at all? Second, if I include it, what should the message be? Regarding the first issue, research provides little comfort as the career experts are often divided as well. Matt, from www.theCampusCareerCoach.com has a good solution. He says, "A good rule of thumb is if you are sending a cover letter, you probably don't need an objective on your resume." Likewise, "If you are not sending a cover letter, you may want to put an objective on your resume." In the end, it really comes down to choice and space. If you have enough room and want to include it, go ahead. The second issue, what to say, is addressed below.

What can an objective statement do for you? Like a great opening line of a book, it can help catch the reader's attention, draw them in, and make them want to read the rest of your story (resume). If you choose to include an objective statement, it should come right after your contact information and help answer the following questions.

- What type of job do you want?
- What skills do you have?
- How will your skills benefit the employer?

The above questions are color-coded to show how each part matches up with the examples listed below in Figure 1.12.

Figure 1.12 - Objective Statement Examples

"To obtain an entry level accounting position *utilizing my educational and internship experiences* that will allow me to immediately contribute to the growth of the company."

"Seeking an administrative position *where my organizational and communication skills* can be fully utilized by your company."

"To obtain a customer service position *that will highlight my experiences, creativity, and people skills* and have an immediate impact with your company."

If you have specific skills (programming languages, accounting software experience, Word/Excel certifications, etc., include these in your objective statement if they are specific to the job you are applying to. It will help to separate you from the competition.

Don't get discouraged if you can't come up with something right away. This can be one of the hardest parts of the resume to write because it requires you to be brief and to the point. It is similar to an elevator speech, discussed later in the book, and a necessity for any prepared job hunter. However, if you take your time, answer the three questions, and make it as succinct as possible, you'll likely draw attention to your resume over someone else.

Step 5: Summary of Qualifications/Executive Profile

If you recently graduated or changed careers, we recommend using an Objective Statement as discussed above. If this is applicable to you, feel free to skip ahead to Step 6 below.

If you do have several years of experience, your Objective Statement should be replaced with a Summary of Qualifications or Executive Profile. These are three to five bullet points or brief statements telling the reader why you are the best candidate for the job. They should be placed at or near the top of the resume, preferably right after your contact information. Like the Objective, the Summary of

Qualifications or Executive Profile needs to answer several key questions about you. We have compiled a sample list of key questions and possible responses:

> Q. How much experience do you have in a particular field or profession?
> A. Highly accomplished CPA with over 10 years of experience in management and accounts receivable.
>
> Q. What qualifications do you have?
> A. Skilled team leader that consistently delivers projects within the allotted time frame and under budget.
>
> Q. What is one great career achievement?
> A. Received the accounting professional of the year award for work on behalf of a local non-profit community.
>
> Q. What is your management or work style?
> A. Extremely motivated and hardworking professional that enjoys new challenges and readily accepts the demands of increasing responsibility.
>
> Q. What are some personal attributes?
> A. Highly skilled in analyzing data and communicating this information both verbally and in writing to a varied audience.

You can format this part of your resume by using either bullet points or a series of short sentences. Figure 1.13 shows the bullet point format and Figure 1.14 shows a series of short sentences.

> **Figure 1.13 - Summary of Qualifications (Bullet Point Format)**
>
> - Highly accomplished CPA with over 10 years of experience in management and accounts receivable.
> - Skilled team leader that consistently delivers projects within the allotted time frame and under budget.
> - Received the accounting professional of the year award for work on behalf of the local non-profit community.
> - Extremely motivated and hardworking professional that enjoys new challenges and readily accepts the demands of increasing responsibility.
> - Highly skilled in analyzing data and communicating this information both verbally and in writing to a varied audience.

> **Figure 1.14 - Summary of Qualifications (Short Sentences)**
>
> Highly accomplished CPA with over 10 years of experience in management and accounts receivable. Skilled team leader that consistently delivers projects within the allotted time frame and under budget. Received the accounting professional of the year award for work on behalf of the local non-profit community. Extremely motivated and hard-working professional that enjoys new challenges and readily accepts the demands of increasing responsibility. Highly skilled in analyzing data and communicating this information both verbally and in writing to a varied audience.

Step 6. Honors and Activities

Extracurricular activities provide a great opportunity to draw attention to your other key attributes and accomplishments. They help:

- Show trends consistent in your life such as leadership and organizational skills.
- Provide a showcase for your values.
- Highlight long-term commitments and dedication to certain causes.
- Show involvement in your local community.
- Reinforce skill sets highlighted previously in your resume.

These may originate from many different areas of your life such as school, work, and community involvement. Below we list some examples.

- Perfect Attendance Award - CBA Community College
- Accounting Award (GPA of 3.8 or higher) - CBA Community College
- Academic Honor Society - CBA Community College
- National Honor Society – Western Prep High School
- Honor Roll – Western Prep High School
- Vice President - York Rotary
- Girl/Boy Scout leader
- Employee of the Month
- Salesperson of the Year

If there is room on your resume, don't be afraid to list these types of activities and accomplishments. They help distinguish you from the competition and give prospective employers better insight into what kind of person you really are.

Step 7: Skills

Include this section in your resume if it is relevant for the job(s) you are applying for by listing:

- Proficiency in certain computer programs. These could be for programs commonly used such as Microsoft Word, Excel, PowerPoint, Access, and QuickBooks. Or, they may be one of the many proprietary systems that are used by a particular business or industry.

- Languages if you speak more than one. Make sure you represent your skill level for each listed language. According to Wikipedia, there are five levels:

- ❖ S-1 or Level 1 - A person at this level can fulfill traveling needs and conduct themselves in a polite manner.

- ❖ S-2 or level 2 - A person at this level is able to satisfy routine social demands and limited work requirements.

- ❖ S-3 or Level 3 - A person at this level is able to speak the language with sufficient structural accuracy and vocabulary to participate effectively in most conversations on practical, social, and professional topics.

- ❖ S-4 or level 4 - A person at this level is able to use the language fluently and accurately on all levels and as normally pertinent to professional needs.

- ❖ S-5 or level 5 - A person at this level has a speaking proficiency equivalent to that of an educated native speaker.

➢ Proficiency with various types of machines and equipment.

Figure 1.15 highlights some of the many types of skills that can be listed on your resume.

Figure 1.15 - Skills

- Microsoft Certifications – Word, Excel, PowerPoint, Access, etc.
- QuickBooks Accounting Software
- Fluent in Spanish (list skill level as noted above)
- Proficient in using a multi-line phone system
- Typing speed - 65 words per minute
- Copying/Scanning/Data Storage

Other skill types such as communication, leadership, interpersonal and problem solving should be integrated into the work experience section of your resume. Rather than just listing these skills by themselves, show how they were used to benefit your previous employers and ultimately your career. Figure 1.16 shows how we incorporated these words into some sample phrases.

> *Figure 1.16 - Other Skills*
>
> - **Problem Solving** - Particularly effective at detecting, diagnosing, and rectifying organizational problems ultimately leading to higher productivity.
>
> - **Interpersonal** - Consistently takes initiative by working to completion on all projects with minimal guidance and supervision.
>
> - **Leadership** - Seeks input and counsel from peers and co-workers before making any departmental decisions or changes.
>
> - **Communication** - Unique ability to develop and maintain relationships within and outside of the organization.

Step 8: References

Unless, you are applying to be a personal assistant, nanny, or something similar, you should not state at the end of your resume that "references are available upon request." However, it is recommended that you prepare a list of references at the same time you are preparing your resume. It should be a separate document and take the following into consideration:

- Include your contact information as well as complete information on your references. To be consistent, use the same contact format as your resume.
- Contact all references for approval before listing their information.
- Keep information current by periodically checking in with your references.
- Send your references a copy of your resume periodically along with a note.
- At a minimum, include at least 3 references that reflect a variety of people, not just managers and co-workers.
- You may need two separate lists for personal and professional references.

Figure 1.17 below shows the proper layout for references.

Figure 1.17 - References

Jane J. Jobseeker
123 Main Street
Anywhereville, PA 12345
(123) 456-7890
jane.jobseeker@email.com

References for Jane J. Jobseeker

Jane Smith
Supervisor, Acme Distributors
321 South Street
Newtown, CA 54321
Work Phone: 111.222.3333
Work Email: js@email.com

John Doe
Controller, Mayfair Industries
123 North Street
Bordertown, CA 65432
Work Phone: 444.555.6666
Work Email: jd@email.com

Fred Newacre
Enrollment Coordinator, YMCA
543 East Street
Somewhereville, NV 66166
Work Phone: 777.888.9999
Work Email: fn@email.com

The Career Puzzle

Your Resume

The Review

Your resume should include all the necessary items mentioned previously along with anything else that can help define and differentiate you from the competition. What it can't contain are mistakes! If it does, your job search will end as quickly as it started. Because it is vitally important to review your work, we suggest doing the following:

> - Save your work. See our previous recommendations under the Tools section regarding the proper procedures.
>
> - Print your resume and proofread for spelling, grammatical, and any other errors.
>
> - Make any revisions or changes on your printed copy.
>
> - Using your printed copy as a guide, make the necessary changes to the electronic version of your resume.
>
> - Repeat Step 2 (Print, Proofread, and Revise) until you feel there are no other changes you can make at this time.
>
> - Once you feel your resume requires no other changes, print it and read out loud. This should be done for two reasons. First, it allows you to hear if the words make sense and sound okay. Second, the interview process is about promoting yourself verbally. The more comfortable you feel speaking about your experiences, the better you'll perform.
>
> - Need any changes after reading your resume? If so, revise, print, review, and continue this process until you feel no other changes can be made. Like the preceding steps, this process may need several repetitions.

Did you know?

The top mistakes job seekers make on their resumes include:

- Hyphen use (e.g. entry-level)

- Verb tense (Led vs. leads, etc.)

- Formatting issues: Make sure your fonts and bullets are the same throughout the resume.

- Education information: Bachelor's Degree vs. Bachelor

- Careless spelling mistakes: The most commonly misspelled words were simple words such as "and"

About.com Job Searching
Alison Doyle

- Now it's time to get a different perspective. Ask others to review your resume and suggest changes. Criticism can be difficult to accept but it will make your resume better. It is far better to find errors now than during the job application process.

- Finally, read over the Rules again listed in this chapter to make sure your resume adheres to each point.

Distribution Methods

Your resume is now ready to meet the world. Instead of having it just sit in a drawer or as a file on your computer where nobody can see it, why not publish it? Below we list various ways to accomplish this.

- Place your resume on your own website or blog. It can be updated or changed quickly, is always available for someone to look at, and attracts the attention of future employers. Some easy ways to accomplish this are by using sites like:
    - Striking.ly https://www.strikingly.com/
    - Visualize.me http://vizualize.me/
    - Resume.com https://www.resume.com/

- Post it on a resume hosting site like Indeed http://www.indeed.com/, VisualCV http://www.visualcv.com/, and Monster.com http://monster.com. These sites allow employers to download your resume in various formats. Make sure you adjust your settings regarding your level of privacy.

- Make your social media sites work even harder and smarter. Sites such as LinkedIn (discussed in a subsequent chapter) and others allow you to post a link to your on-line profile. These sites are quickly becoming the way people find, interact, and collaborate with each other and are beginning to replace the paper resume and business card.

- Keep your resume easily accessible by putting it in the cloud on sites such as Google Docs, Dropbox, ABox and Boxnet. These sites allow you to retrieve your resume from everywhere and share it with anyone.

Your Resume

Examples

We wrap up this chapter by showing you three resumes constructed using all the rules and examples from this chapter.

- Figure 1.18 shows a recent high school graduate with only part-time paid work experience. Relevant coursework is placed right after education to highlight the most important area of our candidate's resume. While the candidate may lack work experience, stressing relevant coursework can provide immediate value to a prospective employer.

- Figure 1.19 shows a recent college graduate with no paid work experience. Skills are placed right after education as these two sections represent the most important areas of our candidate's resume. Despite the lack of work experience, our candidate can provide immediate value to a prospective employer with her computer and accounting skills.

- Figure 1.20 shows a college graduate with several years of work experience. Because this candidate has been in the work force for several years, these experiences and skill sets should be listed first on the resume. While education is important, especially when trying to move up the management ladder, employers place a great deal of weight and importance on experience. Employers want someone that can do the job, with minimal training and guidance. Education is the icing on the cake.

Figure 1.18 - Resume (High School Graduate)

Joan J. Jobseeker
123 Main Street
Anywhereville, PA 12345
(123) 456-7890
jane.jobseeker@email.com

Objective

To obtain an entry level position that utilizes my enthusiasm, technology skills, and determination in allowing me to grow and develop into a valued member of the company.

Education

Western Prep High School, Clarion, PA — www.westprep.edu
College Preparatory — *June 2014*
GPA 3.10/4.00

Relevant High School Coursework

Computer classes that provided an in-depth knowledge of Microsoft Office products (Word I, II, Excel, Access, & Publisher) along with web programming languages (HTML 5 & C++). These classes were complemented with business classes in management, entrepreneurship, and accounting.

Activities

- Yearbook Committee – Helped plan the layout of the book and solicited advertising from local businesses.
- Orchestra member (violin) – Four years. Participated in recitals, concerts, and played at various assisted living facilities.
- Relay for Life – Helped raise funds and participated in the relay event.
- SPCA – Weekly volunteer providing help with the animals, training volunteers, and assisting with adoptions.

Honors/Awards

- Honor Roll
- Perfect Attendance
- Silver Award – Girl Scouts

Experience

Pet-Sitting Services — *2012 - Present*

- Services include all aspects of pet care.
- Responsible for obtaining customers through various marketing activities.
- Profits are used to grow business while also saving for college.

Child Care — *2010 - 2013*

- Provide child care for several local families.

Your Resume

Figure 1.19 - Resume (College Graduate Without Paid Work Experience)

Jane J. Jobseeker
123 Main Street
Anywhereville, PA 12345
(123) 456-7890
jane.jobseeker@email.com

Objective

To obtain an entry level accounting position utilizing my education and internship experiences that will allow me to immediately contribute to the growth of the company.

Education

CBA Community College, Kroy, PA — www.cba.edu
Associate Degree/Computerized Accounting Management — May 2013
GPA 3.8/4.0

Relevant Courses:
- Principles of Accounting I, II, III, IV, V, VI
- Income Tax Preparation I, II
- Payroll Preparation
- Principles of Cost Accounting
- Accounting Information Systems I, II

Skills

- Typing Speed - 70 words per minute
- Mastery of MS Suite of Products (Word, Excel, PowerPoint, Access)
- Experience with accounting software packages (QuickBooks, Peachtree)
- Familiar with several operating systems (Windows, Linux, Mac)

Professional/Work Experience

Administrative Assistant (Six-Week Internship) — April 2013 - May 2013
ABC Accounting — www.abcaccounting.com
Anytown, PA 12345

- Entered, organized, and reviewed data utilized in supervisor's reports
- Assisted in the preparation of financial statements and other related reports
- Performed a variety of administrative duties, including research, fact checking and organizing client files
- Assisted in the reconciliation of accounts receivable/payable and bank statements
- Worked with the finance team on yearly forecasting efforts

Honors and Activities

- Perfect Attendance Award - CBA Community College
- Accounting Award (GPA of 3.8 or higher) - CBA Community College
- Academic Honor Society - CBA Community College
- National Honor Society - Central York High School
- Honor Roll - Central York High School

Figure 1.20 - Resume (College Graduate With Paid Work Experience)

Jane J. Jobseeker
123 Main Street
Anywhereville, PA 12345
(123) 456-7890
jane.jobseeker@email.com

Executive Profile

Skillful and dedicated Executive Assistant with over five years of extensive experience in the support of daily operational and administrative functions

Adept at developing and maintaining detailed administrative and procedural processes that reduce redundancy, improve accuracy and efficiency within budget requirements

Highly focused and results-oriented in supporting complex, deadline-driven operations; able to identify goals and priorities and resolve issues in initial stages

Comfortable working with all levels of colleagues, clients and other external contacts on a variety of projects differing in scope

Extremely Proficient with Microsoft Office Suite (Word, Excel, PowerPoint, Access)

Professional/Work Experience

Executive Assistant — May 2008 - Present
ABC Worldwide — www.abcworldwide.com
Anytown, PA 12347

- Provide a multi-faceted approach in coordinating, organizing, and documenting inter-departmental communication by fully utilizing the company's intranet software
- Enhanced communication between departments and executive team, fostering a sense of teamwork and collaboration
- Negotiated favorable terms and pricing agreements with resorts, vendors, caterers and other providers for service at special events, saving at least $50k annually
- Improved office efficiency by implementing color-coded filing system and introducing additional time-saving measures
- Planned and coordinated PR initiatives, business development events, partner retreats, holiday parties and more

Customer Care Associate — April 2006 - Present
Acme Car Rental (Part-time) — www.acmecars.com
Somewhereville, PA 98765

- Professionally detail interior and exterior of rental cars
- Retrieve and deliver rental cars to various locations
- Train employees on the servicing requirements of all returned vehicles.
- Frequently provide procedural suggestions that enhanced service and resulted in higher profitability

Education

CBA Community College, Kroy, PA — www.cba.edu
Associate Degree/Business Administration Management — May 2008
GPA 3.5/4.0

Honors and Activities

- Rotary - Local Chapter President
- Girl Scouts - Local Leader
- Distinguished Employee of the Month Award

The Career Puzzle

Need more examples? Below are the links to several sites that will provide you with ideas regarding layout and wording:

- http://www.themuse.com/advice/the-41-best-resume-templates-ever
- http://www.indeed.com/resumes
- http://career-advice.monster.com/resumes-cover-letters/resume-samples/sample-resumes-by-industry/article.aspx
- http://susanireland.com/resume/examples/
- http://www.liveresumeexamples.com/

These, and other similar sites, can be used as a guide in helping you write your resume. The key word is help because the finished product must be in your *own* words. Taking the time to figure out just the right words to describe your accomplishments and achievements provides the necessary training needed to verbalize this information during an interview.

The resume is your foot in the door. Once in the door though, you'll want to utilize every resource available in helping you move to the next round. One of the best resources you can use is your portfolio. Discussed in the next chapter, it provides another way in which you can differentiate yourself from the competition.

Chapter 2 – Your Portfolio

"Do something today that your future self will thank you for." - Anonymous -

If you have followed the advice from Chapter 1, you should now be in possession of a resume that has been well thought out, thoroughly reviewed, and ready to meet the world. If that is the case, you are now well equipped to move on to the next step. If that is not the case, we suggest you spend some more time in Chapter 1 perfecting your resume.

The focus of this chapter is about building a valuable resource to assist you during those crucial times (job interview, performance review, entrance interview, etc.) of your career. If you are diligent regarding this process, you will end up with a powerful document that details your past accomplishments and highlights your future capabilities. To help you complete this important undertaking as easily as possible, we have structured the chapter using a question and answer format. To ensure success, we suggest you complete each section before moving on to the next.

What Is It?

Also called a personal portfolio or career portfolio, it is the physical evidence (artifacts) of your experiences (academic, professional, & personal) presented in a cohesive timeline up through the present.

Why Have One?

Whether you are new to the job market, or have several years of experience, you'll need a way to differentiate yourself from other job seekers. The portfolio is that difference and allows you to showcase your accomplishments in a unique way. The process of collecting, gathering and organizing your information into a unifying theme, will help prepare you for future interviews. While a resume helps *tell* a prospective employer about your accomplishments, a portfolio will *show* them how you did it. Jerome Bruner, Syntactic Theory of Visual Communication, reinforced this point when he said, "People will remember 10% of what they hear, 20% of what they read, and 80% of what they see."

Where Should I Start?

To get started, gather every document and artifact related to your past and present academic, professional, and personal accomplishments. Collect everything you can think of even if you are not sure it is relevant and place the items together in a folder, binder, or box. Digital artifacts should be saved and stored in a specific folder on your computer. This is discussed later in the chapter.

What Should Be Included?

The section titled (How Should It Be Organized?) later in this chapter, provides a comprehensive list of items that can be included in your portfolio. Use this list to help gather your artifacts. You won't have every item listed nor will you put everything collected into your portfolio. Your goal at this point is to gather as many items as possible for inclusion.

The stage of your career will greatly influence what your portfolio will look like. If you are a recent high school or college graduate, you will probably have a portfolio skewed more toward your academic achievements. If you are returning to school after a period of time or making a career change, you are more likely to have artifacts that represent professional achievements. Regardless of what point you are at in your career, the key is to show how your past accomplishments directly relate to your future performance. Therefore, it is very important to include items that help document those achievements.

What Shouldn't Be Included?

Do not include anything that is irrelevant, unprofessional, and fails to show you in the best possible light. Therefore do not add the following:

- Items the reader may find confusing
- Damaged looking items
- Things that are not real or verifiable

- Duplicates of any items
- Work that is proprietary in nature
- Items you did not create

How Should It Be Organized?

Hopefully your collection efforts yielded a variety of artifacts from the many different areas of your life. We now move from the collection phase to the sorting phase to determine what goes into your portfolio. You'll want to include items that are relevant as well as being easy to comprehend and follow by the reader. One way is by using the outline listed below. Divided into two main parts, it first introduces you to the reader, and then takes them on a journey that showcases your accomplishments both personally and professionally. Or, use your own format and present the material in a way that best reflects who you are.

Part I

Introduction

- Letter of Introduction (Cover Letter Template) - Discussed at greater length in the section titled What Materials Are Needed?
- Resume – Discussed in Chapter 1
- References – Discussed in Chapter 1
- Letters of Recommendation - Discussed at greater length in the section titled What Materials Are Needed?

Part II

Education

- Diplomas/Certificates, Licenses
- Transcripts
- Course Descriptions/Catalog
- Assessments, Test results
- Writing Samples
- Internships

- Achievement/Awards (Dean's List, Honor Roll, National Honor Society, etc.)
- Brief description of the educational institutions attended
- Training (military, private, business)

Professional Experience

- Apprenticeships
- Special projects
- Workshops, seminars, conferences
- Leadership positions
- Performance reviews, appraisals
- Major projects completed or participated in
- Professional development
- Published articles
- Accomplishments documented (Increased sales, lowered expenses, etc.)
- Samples of work

Community Service

- Volunteer activities
- Organization membership
- Service project participation

Personal Growth

- Independent learning
- Team sport participation
- Hobbies, Interest
- Public Speaking
- Travel

Personal Qualities or Strengths

- Skills, abilities and marketable qualities
- Teamwork
- Contributions to your family
- Raising a family and/or running a household
- Keeping fit
- Managing an illness
- Caregiver for family or friend

As noted previously, don't feel obligated to include everything you have collected. That is the scrapbook approach, will make your portfolio look cluttered, and may overwhelm anyone trying to read it. Rather, be judicious regarding what you include and choose only those items that represent your finest accomplishments and best work. Each item should be unique, meaningful, and provide discussion opportunities that help you stand out during the interview.

If you are pursuing different fields of employment, you will need multiple portfolios (separate portfolios for each field). Some documentation may be used for both but each portfolio must be aligned with the particular field you have chosen to pursue.

Finally, don't stress if you do not have many items. Going forward though, make it a habit to save items that may be of future use. You will change and your portfolio must do the same. Therefore, add to it when the opportunity arises.

What Medium Should I Use?

Carefully consider every item that is to be included in your portfolio. Each must be relevant in its own way and at the same time add to the overall message you are trying to convey. That same deliberation should apply when determining how your materials will be delivered and presented. Depending on your creativity, comfort level, and accessibility to technology, your options include:

1. **Hard copy** – Information stored in a book format.
2. **E-portfolio (off-line)** – Information stored electronically on devices such as a flash drive, computer, tablet, etc.
3. **E-portfolio (on-line)** – Information stored on-line and accessible everywhere.

Below we discuss the advantages and disadvantages of each format.

Hard Copy

One of the easiest and most popular portfolio layouts, the hard copy allows you to assemble your artifacts into a book format that is housed in some type of binder or cover. Options regarding the types of coverings used are discussed more in-depth later in the chapter.

Advantages

- You have control over who sees it, what they see, and when they see it.
- It's a tangible thing that can be touched and held.
- It can be easier to update than other methods depending upon your skill level.

Disadvantages

- It cannot easily be replaced if lost or damaged.
- Artifacts can become worn or damaged.
- It must be consistently updated or it can become irrelevant or look dated.
- You must carry it to every interview.

E-Portfolio (Off-line)

Advantages

- Can be safely stored on a computer, tablet, CD, hard drive, or other external devices.
- Can be easily duplicated or replaced.
- Does not show wear and tear like printed materials.
- Can easily be updated or added to.

Disadvantages

- Software conflicts and file size may cause viewing problems during an interview.
- Access to a computer, tablet, etc. is required during an interview.
- Non-electronic artifacts must be scanned into a computer in order to be added to your portfolio.

E-Portfolio (On-line)

Advantages

- Can be updated easily with changes available immediately.
- Does not show wear and tear like printed materials.
- Can be easily accessed and viewed 24/7/365.
- A link to your website can be sent to prospective employers.

Disadvantages

- Access to a computer is required during an interview.
- Non-electronic artifacts must be scanned into a computer in order to be added to your portfolio.

Did you know?

56% percent of all hiring managers are more impressed by a candidate's personal website than any other branding tool – however, only 7% of job seekers actually have a personal website.

Source: Workfolio

Your Portfolio

> On-line portfolios can be accessed by everyone so privacy issues may be a concern.

While the e-portfolio (off-line or on-line) is increasingly becoming more common, utilize the method you feel most comfortable with in presenting your story.

What Materials Are Needed?

In the preceding section, we discussed three ways to assemble your portfolio: hard copy, e-portfolio (off-line), and e-portfolio (on-line). We now look at each method and the materials needed for each technique.

Hard Copy

Materials

Computer

You'll need one that contains a word processing program like Microsoft Word. Alternatively, you can use other products or one of the many on-line versions discussed previously. See Chapter 1 (Your Resume) under the section on Tools for more information.

Printer

Color if possible but not required. If you don't have access to a printer, many businesses offer printing, copying, and scanning services such as FedEx www.fedex.com, The UPS Store www.theupsstore.com, and Staples www.staples.com. These services can be utilized in person and in most cases on-line.

Scanner

You may have objects that are too precious or unwieldy to include in your portfolio. A scanner will allow you to copy and insert these items into your portfolio as a picture. Many printers are multifunctional (copy, scan, fax) and are relatively inexpensive to purchase. If you do not have access to a scanner, visit one of the locations mentioned above or a local office supply store. They can help you scan your items and save the images to your portable flash drive.

Binders

Shown in Figure 2.1, binders are used for housing and protecting your work. Both functional and stylish, they come in a variety of colors, materials and styles. When choosing, pick a style that does not detract from the contents inside. Unless you are applying for artistic or creative jobs, lean toward a more conservative appearance.

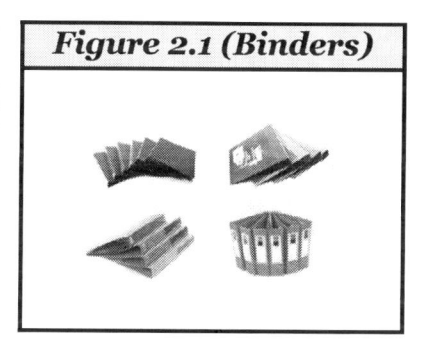

Figure 2.1 (Binders)

Binders of varying widths (thickness of the spine) can be purchased and come in several sizes (1 inch, 1.5 inches, 2 inches, etc.). The key is choosing a size that will hold all your material comfortably. Not too small that it appears crammed together and not too big that it appears unfinished or lacking content. If you use page protectors, which we recommend and are discussed next, a 1-1/2 inch binder should comfortably fit 50 page protectors. That translates to 100 sheets of paper (2 pieces of paper in each protector). Use a different size binder if you have significantly more or less artifacts.

Figure 2.2 (Binder With Pocket)

Rather than just purchasing a plain binder, we recommend one that is functional as well as stylish as shown in Figure 2.2. These binders, containing a pocket in the inside front cover or wrapped in clear plastic, allow you to create your own unique portfolio cover.

Page Protectors

Figure 2.3 (Page Protectors)

Are plastic sleeves or covers that are designed to hold and protect paper from becoming damaged. Figure 2.3 shows a top loading (sheet of paper slips in at the top) page protector. When used correctly, they help protect your artifacts, keep them stationary, and present a unified look throughout your portfolio. They range in thickness/grade from lightweight (economy) to heavy duty. We suggest choosing a grade somewhere in between.

Section Dividers

Figure 2.4 (Page Protector used as a section divider)

Provide a unique way to break up your work into distinct parts (education, professional experience, etc.) making it more organized and readable. Below we list several ways to accomplish this:

1. Type the title of the appropriate section (introduction, education, etc.) on a sheet of paper and place it in a page protector similar to Figure 2.4. This will help the reader know where each section begins and ends. To make it more distinctive, use a paper color other than white. We suggest using the same color throughout, providing a more consistent and cohesive feel to your portfolio.

Figure 2.5 (Page Protector With Tabs)

2. Page protectors with tabs, as shown in Figure 2.5, can be customized (numbered or lettered) and referenced by the index page of your portfolio. Or, you can label the tabs to reflect the contents (education, proofread, community service, etc.) of a particular section.

3. Dividers with tabs that clearly delineate each section of your portfolio as shown in Figure 2.6.

Incorporating any one of the methods listed above will greatly enhance the functionality and appearance of your portfolio.

Figure 2.6 (Section Dividers With Tabs)

Colored Paper

Colored paper, like the one shown in Figure 2.4, can be used in conjunction with page protectors to make your section dividers. We recommend using slightly heavier paper, such as card stock, for the dividers.

Artifacts

Including the best possible items in your portfolio requires careful deliberation during a three phase process of collection, separation, and selection.

Collection

This is the gathering phase. It was discussed previously with suggestions on what to include listed under the section "How Should It Be Organized."

Separation

Once you have collected all your artifacts, you'll need to sort and group them into specific categories. In our example, we have sorted the items by topic (education, professional experience, community service, etc.). There are many different ways to present your artifacts. Use a method that represents you in the best possible way.

Selection

The previous phase (separation) allows you to see what kind of artifacts and how many you have for a particular category. Quality counts over quantity when evaluating the items for inclusion. Fewer high quality artifacts make a much better impression than including many mediocre items. Therefore, choose carefully. Once you have finished this process, you are now ready to begin assembling your portfolio.

Assembling

We have divided this task into two parts, the binder and contents. The bulk of your time and attention will be on focused on getting the information contained in your portfolio just right. However, a portion of your time must be dedicated to protecting and properly housing your valuable artifacts. We'll address this task first.

Binder

Your portfolio binder consists of three outside surfaces, front cover, back cover, and spine. Because the front cover is the most noticeable part of your portfolio, you'll want to concentrate most of your efforts here. If you have the time and inclination, the spine can also be finished while the back cover can be left blank.

Front Cover

Regardless of the style of binder, you'll want to choose one that can be personalized (has a pocket to insert a sheet of paper). To make the front cover, print the title, your name, and center it on the page about a third of the way down from the top as shown in Figure 2.7. Feel free to print your information on a color other than white. When inserted into your binder, it should look like your very own book cover.

Figure 2.7 - Front Cover

Professional Portfolio

for

Jane J. Jobseeker

Spine

If your binder contains a pocket on the spine, feel free to use this space as an additional identifier. We used the same information from our front cover and modified it for the smaller space as shown below in Figure 2.8. You'll need to cut your paper to the proper size so that it will easily slide into the spine pocket. We recommend using the same color paper used for your front cover.

Figure 2.8 - (Spine Cover)

PORTFOLIO FOR JANE J. JOBSEEKER

While the materials for your binder can be obtained from many different stores, we suggest purchasing them from a place that specializes in office supplies. It may not be the cheapest option, but it will generally provide a much larger selection of higher quality materials from which to choose.

Contents

To be consistent, our discussion will follow the layout previously listed under "How Should It Be Organized?"

Operational Tips

Two artifacts can be placed back to back in a single page protector providing a more panoramic view of your work.

Make a copy or take a picture of any artifacts that may be too small, large, or oddly shaped to fit neatly into a page protector. For these types of items, you can:

- ➢ Integrate pictures into your narrative.
- ➢ Attach them to a sheet of paper and insert into a page protector.
- ➢ Place them in the pockets located in the inside front and back covers of many binders.

When you are finished placing the artifacts in the page protectors, place them in piles that correspond to the different sections of your portfolio (education, professional, community service, etc.) or according to your layout method.

Cover Page

Because the binder cover identifies you as the owner and author of the portfolio, you do not have to include a cover page. However, you can replicate the binder cover and insert it here if you wish. If not, your first page would be the index. If you choose to leave your binder cover blank, include a cover page that is similar to the front cover discussed above.

Your Portfolio

Index

This provides the reader with a quick synopsis of what your portfolio contains and where specific information is located. Ideally, your page numbers should correspond to the items in your index. Figure 2.9 shows an index that is numerical. Unfortunately, we realize it can be difficult, if not impossible, to place page numbers on many of your artifacts. One way around this dilemma is to use binder tabs as shown above. While they do not reference specific pages, they do allow you to narrow your search to a pertinent section of your portfolio.

The second index example below, Figure 2.10, is based on dividing your portfolio into sections. Because you won't know the exact contents of your portfolio until it is finished, complete the index last.

Figure 2.9 - Index (Numerical)

Index

Introduction Letter	Page 1
Resume	Page 2
References	Page 3
Letters of Recommendation	Page 4
Education	Page 5
Work Experience	Page 6
Community Service	Page 7
Personal Growth	Page 8
Personal Qualities or Strengths	Page 9

> **Figure 2.10 - Index (Sections)**
>
> # Index
>
> | | |
> |---|---|
> | Introduction Letter | Section 1 |
> | Resume | Section 1 |
> | References | Section 1 |
> | Letters of Recommendation | Section 1 |
> | | |
> | Education | Section 2 |
> | Work Experience | Section 3 |
> | Community Service | Section 4 |
> | Personal Growth | Section 5 |
> | Personal Qualities or Strengths | Section 6 |

Introduction Letter

Your portfolio, like your resume, is at its best when it's in front of many people in a variety of different situations (hiring, performance reviews, promotions, etc.) Just like the resume, your portfolio needs an introduction. While it can't be written for any specific employer or particular job, it still must provide the reader with an overall summary of who you are. You may be able to use some of this information in your cover letter, modified accordingly, when applying for specific jobs. Figure 2.11 shows the basic form of a cover letter template and the contents each paragraph should contain. Figure 2.12 shows what an actual portfolio cover letter may look like.

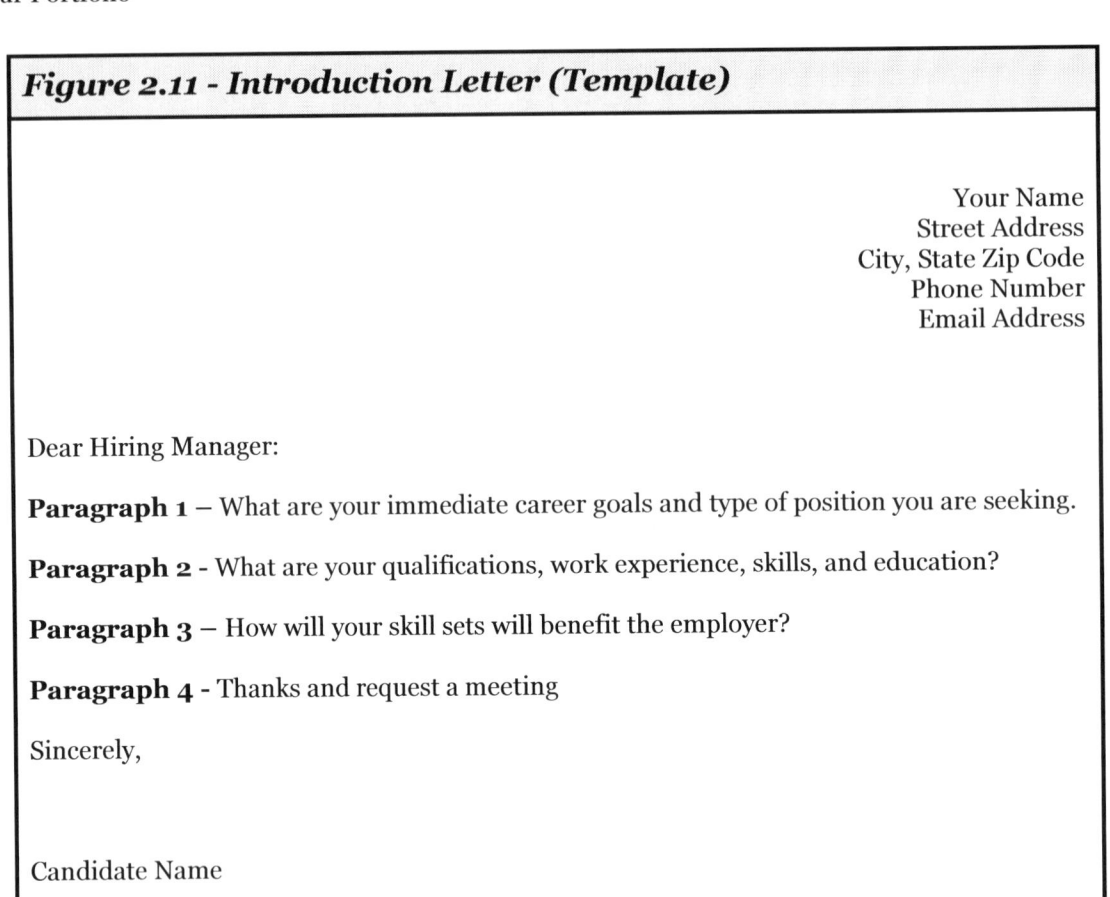

Figure 2.11 - Introduction Letter (Template)

Your Name
Street Address
City, State Zip Code
Phone Number
Email Address

Dear Hiring Manager:

Paragraph 1 – What are your immediate career goals and type of position you are seeking.

Paragraph 2 - What are your qualifications, work experience, skills, and education?

Paragraph 3 – How will your skill sets will benefit the employer?

Paragraph 4 - Thanks and request a meeting

Sincerely,

Candidate Name

Enclosures

Figure 2.12 - Introduction Letter (Sample)

Jane J. Jobseeker
123 Main Street
Anywhereville, PA 12345
(123) 456-7890
jane.jobseeker@email.com

Dear Hiring Manager:

As a recent graduate with honors, I am seeking to join an organization that will allow me to utilize my skills in accounting and technology to make an immediate impact.

After completing my Associates Degree in Computerized Accounting, I have recently enrolled in a continuing professional education program sponsored by the American Institute of CPAs to further enhance my credentials in the field.

My education and subsequent internship experiences have allowed me to develop a wide range of skills and qualities. These include:

- A solid foundation in technology (Microsoft Word, Excel, PowerPoint, Access) that allow me to not only extract information but apply it in solving problems and answering questions.

- The ability to effectively communicate ideas in a clear, concise, and logical manner. This is coupled with a track record of dependability and reliability proven by my awards for outstanding attendance.

- As president of the Student Association, I was able to inspire, motivate, and move others toward a specific goal.

Thank you for your time and review of my credentials. If you would like to discuss my qualifications in person, I can be reached at (123) 456-7890 or jane.jobseeker@email.com.

Sincerely,

Jane Jobseeker

Enclosures

Resume

Discussed in Chapter 1

References

Discussed in Chapter 1

Letters of Recommendation

It is highly recommended that you get one or more people to write letters of recommendation on your behalf. These testimonials help build and reinforce your brand and can often be the deciding factor between you and your competition. There are many individuals you can ask including teachers, coaches, advisors, managers, supervisors, co-workers, and others.

To make this process go as smoothly as possible:

- Ask someone that knows you well, not just because they are important.
- Tell them why they would be good person to write a letter on your behalf.
- Give them plenty of time and provide a deadline if necessary.
- Think about giving them a template or examples that can be modified.

The writer of a recommendation letter should include the following four things:

1. How they know the person and length of the relationship.
2. Describe the skills, accomplishments, and traits of the individual. Provide specific examples if possible.
3. Summarize why the candidate should be hired.
4. Offer to provide more information if needed by including a phone number and email address.

Education

List your most recent artifacts first. Items to include are:

- **Educational Institution(s)** - Provide a brief description of the schools you attended.

- **Diplomas, certificates, and licenses** - For security and safety, we recommend using copies of any official documents to prevent possible damage and loss.

- **Transcripts** - Are a great way to give a prospective employer a quick overview of your educational experiences. However, they may end up working against you if any grades received were less than a "B". If so, or your overall grade point average is just average, we suggest omitting these from your portfolio.

- **Course Descriptions/Catalog** - Make sure to highlight any courses that are relevant or key to the job or industry that you are interviewing for.

- **Assessments/Test results** - Include any certifications attained as part of your educational training.

- **Writing Samples** - As noted earlier in this book, employers are keen to hire candidates that can communicate effectively. If possible, show samples of your writing. They can take many forms such as letters, reports, research or projects that you completed or collaborated on.

- **Achievement/Awards** (Dean's List, Honor Roll, National Honor Society, etc.) - While these awards and achievements mainly highlight your academic prowess, they also provide insight into your work ethic. Additionally, they help separate you from other candidates and are a great indicator of your commitment to learning.

- **Training** (military, private, business) - Shows initiative and willingness to change and adapt over time. Therefore, list any activities, certificates, and time spent in pursuit of self-improvement.

Work Experience

Include artifacts from your most recent employment experience first and any previous employment experiences, if applicable. You may not have artifacts for every place you ever worked. That's where your resume comes to the rescue by making up for what your portfolio lacks. They should complement each other with one telling what you did and the other showing how you did it. Refer back to the section "How Should it be Organized?" under the section Professional Experience for ideas regarding what to include.

Personal Development

appear involving community service, personal growth, and personal qualities or strengths should be included in this section. These types of items allow you to establish a more complete picture of yourself and help show patterns of behavior that are consistent, regardless of whether they are professional or personal.

Your artifacts may be represented in a variety of different ways and will likely consist of:

- **Tangible** - Objects, pictures, official documents, letters, and other items. If these are not self-explanatory, label or describe the artifact in a few sentences.

- **Intangible** - Items like activities, personal qualities, or experiences. While you can write about these, try and bring them to life with a visual representation. Pictures will help captivate the reader and stimulate the conversation.

Regardless of the format, make sure your artifacts are properly represented on the pages of your portfolio.

Electronic – Off-line

Materials

Computer & Scanner

This information was discussed earlier in this chapter.

Software

This information was discussed earlier in this chapter.

Flash Drive, CD, or DVD

Discussed in Chapter 1, these tools provide portable storage for your work and can safeguard against any losses.

Assembling

If you are not enamored about carrying your portfolio binder to every interview, you may want to use a digital format instead. Along with making it portable, it allows you to store and show your work on a variety of devices such as a computer, laptop or tablet. To make a digital version, you'll need to do the following steps:

1. **Finalize** all artifacts to be included in your e-portfolio.

2. **Create** a file folder on your computer called e-portfolio. This will be the repository for all your scanned documents, pictures and files.

3. **Scan** any artifacts into the computer that are not already in digital format. To do this, you'll need a computer with a scanner attached to it. When scanning, save each artifact using a unique name and place it in the e-portfolio folder. If any artifacts are three-dimensional or too large to scan, take a picture of the item and save it in the e-portfolio folder.

4. **Open** a new document in a word processor such as Microsoft Word. This is where you will construct your portfolio and import your artifacts.

5. **Assembling/Organizing** - Your e-portfolio can be made to look just like a hard copy stored in a binder. Utilizing our template from the section "How Should it be Organized?" the layout of your e-portfolio would include the following:

   - Title Page
   - Introduction Letter
   - Index
   - Resume
   - References
   - Letters of recommendation
   - Education Title Page - followed by artifacts
   - Work Experiences Title Page - followed by artifacts
   - Personal Growth - followed by artifacts

   The first page of your word document will be your title page and can look just like the example shown above for the hard copy format. Or, use another type of design.

   Start a new page in the same document and type your introduction letter. Continue this process until all your sections are complete.

6. **Finalizing/Saving** - Make sure you save your work on a periodic basis in your e-portfolio file.

7. **Converting** – When you are satisfied that your portfolio is complete, we suggest converting your document to a PDF file. Per Wikipedia, "Portable Document Format (PDF) is a file format used to represent *documents* in a manner independent of application software, hardware, and operating systems." Meaning, once converted, it will look the same regardless of what type of device it is shown on. Most, if not all, word processing programs allow you to convert your document to a PDF file.

Once converted, save the file to your e-portfolio folder. PDF files cannot be changed unless you obtain editing software. This can be very expensive. Therefore, any updates to your e-portfolio should be done in your word document and then re-saved to a new PDF file for presentation purposes.

The layout of your portfolio is your choice. Keep it organized, be consistent, and above all make it the best representation of you as possible.

Electronic – On-line

Materials

Computer & Scanner

This information was discussed earlier in this chapter.

Website

For presentation of your work.

Assembling

Putting your portfolio on-line, in the form of your own website, makes it immediately accessible for viewing 24/7. Forget about having to carry it around on a CD, memory stick or computer, as it can be viewed anytime, anywhere with just one click.

The steps to get your portfolio on-line are similar to those needed to create an electronic portfolio noted above. However, there are a few minor differences as shown below:

1. **Finalize** all artifacts to be included in your e-portfolio.

2. **Create** a file folder called e-portfolio. This will be the repository for all your scanned documents, pictures and files.

3. **Scan** your artifacts into the computer. See Step 2 under Electronic – Off-line regarding how to get this information into your computer.

4. **Create** a website where your portfolio will reside on-line. Sites like http://wordpress.com/ and http://www.weebly.com/ are free. Or, use a site like www.workfolio.com that is easy to use, helps you quickly build a

site but charges a small fee per month. The key is to choose a site you are comfortable setting up, maintaining, and updating.

5. **Organizing** your on-line portfolio into a compelling website is limited only by your creativity. To make it as professional as possible you'll want to create different pages that tell your story. We suggest including some or all of the following pages on your website:

    - Home
    - About me
    - Resume
    - Samples/Relevant Projects
    - Skills
    - Awards
    - Contact

Upload your information from your e-portfolio folder to the relevant pages. You can have as many pages as you want on your website. However, your goal is to get someone's interest and keep it. Therefore, try and make it succinct, compelling and around four to five pages in length.

It is a great way for companies to find out more about you than just relying on your resume. To get a better idea of what an on-line e-portfolio looks like, check out the links below:

http://portfolios.music.ufl.edu/picclef/

http://www.udel.edu/fth/RachelLeibrandtPortfolio/

http://www.angelfire.com/planet/josie19966/

https://sites.google.com/a/g.clemson.edu/carterw/home

https://sites.google.com/a/g.clemson.edu/katharine-amalfitano/home

http://zrjames.wix.com/eportfolio

What Are My Resources?

Not sure where to begin? Need help? The type of support available will vary depending upon what stage you are at in your career.

High School

If you have not graduated, contact your guidance counselor regarding classes or resources that can assist you in this process. It is never too soon to begin documenting your experiences. A portfolio can help you get a job or gain acceptance into college, the military, or another training program.

College

Regardless of whether you have taken a few classes or received a degree, you are entitled to utilize the resources of the career center of any college you previously attended. These career centers are staffed with trained individuals that can help you with:

- Your portfolio
- Your resume
- Career advice and counseling
- Internship and job search
- Volunteer opportunities

Along with items too numerous to list here, these types of services are at your disposal. Use them to your advantage.

Other

If the above are not applicable, check out your local state employment agency. They offer a variety of programs and resources such as vocational assessment, training, resume creation, and much more.

The Career Puzzle

How Do I Use My Portfolio?

As noted previously, your portfolio can take many forms and be organized in a variety of ways. Choose the method you feel most comfortable with and the one that will best showcase your talents. The format you choose will determine how your portfolio is used during an interview. Below we look at each method and the best way to incorporate your portfolio into the interview process.

Hardcopy

Assembling your artifacts into a binder that details your educational and professional journey is a very satisfying process. When finished, you'll have a portable display that you can proudly hold in your hands. By putting it together with the utmost care and thought, it gives you keen insight regarding where everything is located. This is especially important during an interview. We suggest doing the following with your portfolio binder:

- **Bring** it to every interview. This will get you in the habit of using this valuable resource.

- **Show** examples of your work when the opportunity arises.

- **Attempt** to steer the conversation toward those areas in your book you want to highlight.

- **Allow** the interviewer to look at your book in its entirety. Provide commentary where possible as they peruse your work.

- **Don't** allow anyone to borrow your book. Instead, make copies of specific items if requested.

Your portfolio, in hardcopy format, *helps* tell a story by using tangible evidence regarding your accomplishments. It is not meant to speak for itself or be a replacement for you during an interview. Rather, its function is to be a reference that displays your past and provides an indicator of future performance. Therefore, bring this document into the conversation to show why you are the most qualified candidate.

Electronic – Off-line

The e-portfolio is becoming much more common as technology makes it easier than ever to showcase your talents digitally. While the form and appearance of an e-portfolio may differ from the binder format, its role is the same. Along with the suggestions noted above regarding the hardcopy version, we recommend the following for your e-portfolio:

- **Save** your work in a variety of places for safekeeping. For example, keep a copy on your laptop or desktop along with a copy saved on a portable device such as USB flash drive.

- **Bring** a device (laptop, tablet) to the interview to show your work, if possible. You may not have access to a computer unless one is provided. If you do not have a computer for use during the interview, save your work to a format (such as a PDF file) that will change little when viewed on different machines.

- **Prepare** your computer and e-portfolio ahead of time so you can access and show the information quickly and easily. Make sure your device is fully charged and your documents are ready for viewing.

- **Don't** send a copy of your work prior to the interview but instead use as needed to get your points across.

- **Refrain** from giving a copy to the interviewer unless you are hired.

Electronic – On-line

Placing your portfolio permanently on-line is the ultimate step in making it accessible to everyone all the time. Because of this, it must be used and constructed differently than the two methods discussed previously. Therefore, we recommend the following:

- **Tell** your story. Your portfolio has to do this on its own because you may not be available to help navigate the viewer through your work.

- **Make** each page unique and keep the website to around four or five pages total.

- ➢ **Use** an email address for your contact information. Keep it separate from your personal information. Otherwise, you may be solicited and receive many unwanted emails.

- ➢ **Don't** include a phone number on your website.

- ➢ **Bring** a device that allows you to access your website during the interview. If that is not possible, have the address readily available for the interviewer.

- ➢ **Forward** a link to your website to the person(s) you interviewed with. This is a great way to follow-up and keep your name in the forefront.

Time spent working on your portfolio equals time spent preparing for future interviews. Interviews provide the opportunity to align your experiences and strengths to a particular job. The portfolio supports this process by showing prospective employers how your past actions are indicative of future behaviors.

Should I Add To My Portfolio?

Yes! Your portfolio is a representation of your past to be used in the present to gain employment in the future. Because the future holds change for your career, your portfolio must change along with it. Therefore, get in the habit of consistently updating your portfolio by adding relevant artifacts of your experiences. There are several ways to do this. You can simply add content to the applicable sections of your portfolio. Or, you can move forward by:

1. **Constructing a new portfolio**. After landing your first job after high school or college, start fresh with a new binder. This allows your focus to be exclusively on accumulating professional artifacts going forward.

2. **Dividing your portfolio.** Segregate it into sections that correspond with the major segments of your life such as high school, college, and any professional endeavors. As your career matures, your most recent accomplishments will focus on your current skill sets and should dominate the conversation.

3. **Using a streamlined approach.** Use only the best artifacts from your past educational, personal, and professional experiences. Add to each section as the opportunity arises.

Regardless how you choose to organize your portfolio, the important thing is to keep it up to date. Your resume has to be current. Extend the same courtesy to your portfolio and you will be rewarded for your efforts.

To summarize, the portfolio:

- Allows you to be different from your competition. Very few job seekers take the time to construct a portfolio providing you with a distinct advantage.

- Gives you the ability to cite specific challenges from your past and the actions taken in surmounting those problems.

- Helps you control the interview by directing the conversation toward those topics that highlight your achievements.

- Can include visuals such as pictures and/or video whereas your resume can't.

- Gets you in the habit of documenting your work. Content can be added to your portfolio and used during performance reviews to show the value you bring to the company. Once completed, it takes minimal effort and time to keep it updated.

Don't be afraid to document and show your accomplishments. If you don't, who will?

Chapter 3 – Your Education

"The whole purpose of education is to turn mirrors into windows." - Sydney J. Harris -

The information age is upon us, transforming the way we work, learn, and play. What's the catalyst for this change? Technology! It's caused an unprecedented upheaval, providing unlimited opportunities to those embracing it, and a life of constant disruption for those who don't. Companies are acutely aware of this and are constantly looking for employees to help them gain an edge in this ever changing global economy. An economy demands lean operations and greater responsibility from everyone. In theory, each employee has to be efficient, flexible, and comfortable with innovation and change. In reality, it means a workforce of critical thinkers applying today's technology to solve future problems.

How can a company be sure you are the right person to help them compete in this fast paced global economy? For starters, utilizing the information discussed in this book will go a long way to create an impressive professional profile. Done correctly your:

Resume   **Cover Letter**

Portfolio

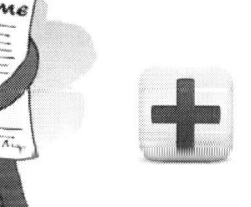

will help convince prospective employers you are a dedicated, passionate, and action-oriented person. But is that enough? Is there something holding you back? Is your lack of formal education hindering your ability to get the jobs you want and deserve? Would a degree, industry certifications, or license bolster your chances? All things being equal, employers will often choose the candidate with more formal education. Credentials matter as employers believe more education often translates into better communication skills, a highly prized commodity in this fast paced information-driven world.

In this chapter, we'll break education into two major categories, formal and informal learning. We look at the reasons and processes of each to show why education is so important to your personal and professional life.

Formal Learning

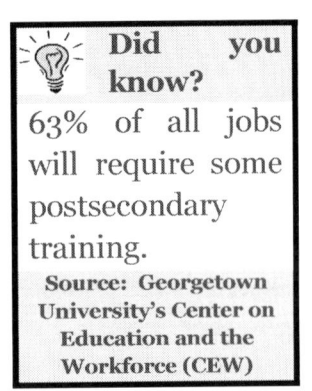

> **Did you know?**
> 63% of all jobs will require some postsecondary training.
> Source: Georgetown University's Center on Education and the Workforce (CEW)

Formal learning is defined as education or training offered by an institution that results in a recognized diploma or certificate. If you have graduated high school, or soon will, that means at least 12 years of your life have been devoted to learning in some type of a formalized setting.

Have you ever wondered why everyone must go through this process? Why public schools were set up in the first place? It originated from the early beginnings of our country as the founding fathers realized the importance of education. They knew the fragile nature of democracy was dependent upon citizens making informed and educated decisions. Because democracy is the rule of the people by the people, it would take an educated populace to rule effectively and fairly. Thomas Jefferson put it more eloquently when he said, *"Educate and inform the whole mass of the people... They are the only sure reliance for the preservation of our liberty."* Digging a bit deeper, they also realized the important contributions each of us make to society, ourselves and each other. John Adams summed it up neatly when he said, *"There are two educations. One should teach us how to make a living and the other how to live."* Because of the educational foundations set up long ago, we are the beneficiaries of a vast array of opportunities that would astound our founders.

The Reasons

Aside from the important historical contexts noted previously, the compelling reasons to further your education are:

Interests

When used properly, education can provide a clear roadmap toward the achievement of your goals and objectives while satisfying your passions. Ask successful business owners why they started their company. For most, if not all, it's less about money and more about the passion of bringing a unique product or service to the marketplace. Focused determination provides the underlying catalyst for achieving success. This same concept applies to your education. Go for the right reasons and not just because someone else expects it of you. Many people attend college, graduate, and work in a job or field they despise and hate. The workforce is filled with unhappy people who would love to be doing something else. Don't let this happen to you.

For the majority of your formal schooling, kindergarten through 12th grade, decisions regarding what you learned were made by people other than yourself (teachers, administrators and parents). These advocates looked out for your best interests. Now, it's your turn. Find your passion and let it help guide you in making the right career decisions.

If you are not exactly sure what you want to do, you'll need to do some research. We discuss this more in-depth in the next section titled "The Process". It is highly recommended that you take the time now to learn more about yourself, your interests, and how they match up to possible careers. Skipping this step or not taking the proper amount of time to really investigate all the possibilities can lead to an unfulfilled life. Don't let this happen to you!

Opportunity Costs

The New Oxford American Dictionary defines Opportunity Cost as, "The loss of potential gain from other alternatives when one alternative has been chosen." In other words, for every opportunity you pursue, there are one or more opportunities that cannot be pursued. For instance, if you decide to continue your education on a full-time basis, your ability to earn money during that period is compromised due to the obligations associated with school (attending class, studying, etc.). This is a tradeoff many make in the hope an advanced degree will increase future earning power and make up for any losses in the short-term. Know and compare your options!

Money

The ability to earn more money is a great motivator for pursuing more education, and for good reason. A report by The Alliance for Excellence in Education shows that "Those that Learn More, Earn More." Their research noted the following:

- $19,540 - Average annual income for a high school dropout in 2009
- $27,380 - Average annual income for a high school graduate in 2009
- $36,190 - Average annual income for an Associate's Degree in 2009
- $46,930 - Average annual income for a Bachelor's Degree in 2009

Over a 40-year career, the total amount earned for each category listed above is shown below in Figure 3.1.

Figure 3.1 (career earnings*)

High School Dropout	High School Graduate	Associate's Degree	Bachelor's Degree
$781,600	$1,095,200	$1,447,600	$1,877,200

* Assumes no change in salary over a 40-year period.

If you have graduated high school, congratulations! That achievement alone will help you earn over $300,000 more in your lifetime versus your non-graduating peers. If you didn't graduate, think very seriously about getting a diploma or its equivalency as soon as possible. You are at a competitive disadvantage and your earning power will be severely limited. The following website provides a step-by-step approach to help you pass the GED (General Educational Development) exam:

http://education-portal.com/articles/How_to_get_a_GED_a_Step-by-Step_Process_to_Earn_a_GED.html

Don't sell yourself short by not finishing high school as the ramifications on your life, personally, professionally, and financially can be enormous.

Just two years of college (an associate's degree) will boost your lifetime earnings to about a million and a half dollars and a four-year (bachelor's) degree gets you closer to two million dollars in lifetime earnings. The increase in earning potential, along with enhanced mobility discussed in the next section, should hopefully provide the motivation you need to take action.

Mobility

Per the Free Dictionary http://www.thefreedictionary.com, mobility is defined as "the movement of people, as from one social group, class, or level to another."

With that in mind, "visualize yourself, along with many other people, in front of 5 doors that have a 1, 2, 3, 4, or 5 painted on each. A higher number means more job opportunities than a lower number. A voice somewhere above says, "If you have a Master's Degree, you may enter door 5 or any door that has a lower number." After a short pause, the voice says, "If you have a Bachelor's Degree, you may enter door 4 or any door that has a lower number." Again, after another short pause, the voice says, "If you have an Associate's Degree, you may enter door 3 or any door that has a lower number." You guessed it, another short pause and the voice says, "If you have a high school degree, you may enter door 2 or any door that has a lower number." What's left? The person with no high school diploma can only go through door 1. Depending upon your education level, the above scenario is either a dream or nightmare.

Three things stand out from the example noted above:

> - The person with a Master's Degree can go through all five, or 100% of the doors. The person with no high school diploma can only go through one, or 20% of the doors, and therefore has limited opportunity and mobility in the workforce.

Did you know?

Research indicates that through 2012, about 44% of young, working college graduates were underemployed and the quality of jobs held by those underemployed has declined, with today's recent graduates increasingly accepting low wage jobs or part-time work, sometimes pushing other low-skilled workers out of the labor market.

Source: http://www.newyorkfed.org/research/current_issues/ci20-1.pdf

> Competition increases with decreasing education. The person without a high school diploma is in competition with everyone else. When the economy is not doing well, individuals with greater educational credentials are often forced to go through lower-numbered doors than they normally would. This limits jobs and suppresses wages for those with less formal education.

> Most, if not all, jobs require a combination of experience and education. Those with lesser educational credentials will often not be considered despite having necessary job experience.

Communications Skills

While most jobs initially depend on your ability to perform various technical tasks, it will be your communication skills that determine how far you advance in your career. Upward movement into the management hierarchy of a company places greater emphasis on your ability to communicate effectively and less on your ability to perform certain technical tasks. Employers are keenly aware that college graduates will likely have better communication skills than their lesser educated peers. This is largely due to additional time spent on writing and speaking while pursuing a post-secondary education. Good communication skills are highly valued and necessary to successfully compete in a global, digital economy.

Improves Well-Being

Previous studies provide a correlation between education, income level and a person's health. The Centers for Disease Control report that people with a bachelor's degree or higher live about nine years longer than those who didn't graduate from high school. Also, those with a higher education level and income were less likely to report health problems than those with less education. Good health allows you to operate at maximum efficiency and navigate the rigors of life. This topic is discussed more in-depth in Chapter 6.

Networking

Networking is how business gets done. Companies would much rather hire applicants that come with recommendations than take a chance on a stranger. Attending college immediately increases your network in several ways. First, you will meet and interact with many different people who are motivated to succeed. Second, you will work closely with students, staff, and faculty in differing circumstances and settings. Finally, you'll become part of an alumni network that can have far-reaching influence. While most of these relationships may initially be forged through friendships in a temporary setting, they can often have lasting importance in regard to your career. Your acquaintances, friends, and alumni will eventually make up a very large network of people in the workforce. This network can help form powerful alliances. Therefore, treat every interaction in your daily life with care.

Resources

As you can see, furthering your education has many advantages. One great benefit that cannot be overlooked is career services. This department can provide a great deal of guidance during your college years and help become your gateway into the working world. This department knows the latest hiring trends, employer needs, and skill sets for success. More about how to use this department effectively is discussed in greater detail below.

> **Did you know?**
> Only 29% of students use their college's career office
> Source: Millennial Branding, a Gen Y research and consulting firm and StudentAdvisor.com

The Process

While the evidence seems overwhelming in support of continuing education, you'll want to carefully determine if it is right for you. Thanks to the Internet, it's easier than ever to research possible careers, schools, along with the educational requirements associated with specific programs of study. While technology constantly disrupts how we do things, it also provides opportunities that were unthinkable just a few years ago. Education is no exception, as it is now accessible to more people than ever before due to the availability of on-line, on-campus, and blended approaches used by many institutions. Because education can now be delivered in a variety of ways, times, and locations, it is important to find out what will work best for you. Before rushing into anything, we suggest you go through the following steps:

Step 1 - Why go to school?

While the reasons listed in the previous section make a pretty compelling argument for furthering your education, does it personally make sense for you? Big decisions, like going/returning to school, require self-examination and will go a long way in helping you make the right decisions. Ask yourself questions like the following:

- Will it help me get a better job?
- Is it needed to advance in my current job?
- Am I really doing what I want to do?
- Am I bored with my job or chosen career?
- Can I reach my potential or dream job without additional education?
- Is it time to try something different?

Whatever the reason, just realizing something may have to change in order to accomplish your goals is a step in the right direction.

Step 2 – What are your interests?

Not sure what is out there or what you want to do? A good place to start is by going to the Department of Education's student aid website at http://studentaid.ed.gov/prepare-for-college/careers. It contains a career search tool that will match your interests with possible careers. From there, you can find out:

- The type and amount of education needed for specific occupations.
- What type of training and schools are located in your area.
- The tuition and fees associated with each program.
- How to finance your education, if necessary.

Take your time and thoroughly investigate all possibilities. Eventually, you'll want to narrow your choices and focus on a few options.

Step 3 - Evaluating your responsibilities

Do you have enough time to be a successful student? What are your obligations during the day – work, kids, caring for parents? Whether you go full-time or part-time, school is demanding at any age. A general rule of thumb is that you'll need to study at least 2-3 hours for every hour of class you attend. Just taking one 3-hour class during the week can translate into 6-9 hours of studying. Taking into account travel time to and from class plus studying could result in approximately 15 hours per week. That's just for one class!

Step 4 - Evaluating your support system

Will family members be able to pick up the slack while you devote time to classes and studying? Great endeavors usually require sacrifice from friends and family. Does everyone know what is involved? How long it will last? What will be the responsibilities for each family member during this time? Getting this out in the open and resolved prior to starting will help minimize misunderstandings.

Step 5 - Career Research

In Step 2 (Your Interests) we recommended doing some research on possible career choices using the Internet. Now it's time to take it a step further by getting a better picture of what certain jobs entail. That means finding someone that does what you want to do. Start by asking family, friends, and acquaintances. If they don't have experience in the areas you are interested in, they probably know someone who does.

Before speaking to others about their job experiences, prepare some questions ahead of time. We listed some below to help you get started.

- ➢ What do you do in a typical day?
- ➢ How did you get into this field?
- ➢ What kind of education, certifications, and skill sets are needed for this job?
- ➢ What are the least and most rewarding aspects of your job?

Your Education

> Would you choose this career again if you started over?

Comparing this information along with your other research will be invaluable in helping you gain insight and first-hand knowledge of what is expected regarding various jobs.

If you can't find someone to talk to, contact a school that offers the program(s) you are interested in. Speak to a counselor in career services. They can help:

> Confirm the program of study needed to reach your goals and any required prerequisites.
> Put you in touch with professionals of your chosen field of study.
> Advise you on financial requirements of the various degrees and training programs.

More importantly, career services should be able to provide information on the success rate of their graduates obtaining employment as well as hiring trends for specific areas of study.

Actually, career services should be the first department you speak with prior to attending any institution. Their willingness to work with you before, during, and after is a good indicator of the school's commitment to its students. Therefore, spend some time with them before starting any program. Carefully evaluating each school and the programs they offer, along with their support system, will allow you to begin narrowing your choices.

Step 6 - Where should I go to school?

Your research in the previous steps may have already answered this question. If not, it can be looked at logically.

> Check to see what institutions in your area offer the programs of study based upon your prior research. College websites should provide the programs and course offerings for the various areas of study. Like what you see? Plan a visit to the school(s).

> If there are no local options, how about on-line? Technology has made this easier than ever as on-line courses can now be taken from hundreds, if not thousands, of colleges in the U.S. and even abroad.

Regardless of where you attend, speak to an admissions representative and a career counselor due to the reasons noted above. Ask them tough questions like:

- What percentage of graduates find jobs after graduating?
- What percentage of graduates find jobs in their field of study?
- What percentage of students graduate in the allotted time frame (2 years, for an associate's degree, 4 years for a bachelor's degree)?
- What is the total cost of attendance including textbooks, fees, tuition, and housing?
- If I take loans, what will be my estimated payments when I graduate?

Sadly, these types of questions are infrequently asked. Believe it or not, many college graduates have buyer's remorse. They have degrees but are unable to find a job applicable to their educational background. Or even worse, they never graduate and are saddled with debt with nothing to show for it. Make sure you know what the college offers, the costs associated with attending, and the prospects for employment after graduating. Spend the time now researching your options in order to minimize any surprises later.

Step 7 - Can you afford it?

Perhaps the most important question you should ask yourself is, "How do I pay for my education? Working part-time? Gifts or loans from family, friends, and relatives? If these options are not available, use the following link to find out more information regarding scholarships, grants, loans, work-study, etc.

http://studentaid.ed.gov/types

Loans may allow you to attend college now but turn into future obligations that can lead to financial hardship. Do whatever it takes to lessen the financial burden of college. Ask yourself, "What is my cheapest option that allows me to get the training I need to advance my career and make more money?" Like everything in life, this boils down to a cost/benefit analysis. Attending school is no different. Specifically, do I *benefit* (get the job I want) based on the *costs* (debt) that I incur?

> **Did you know?**
> Seven in ten college seniors who graduated in 2012 had student loan debt, with an average of $29,400 for those with loans.
> http://www.ticas.org/

Your Education

What does it take to pay off $29,400 in school loans? Check out Figure 3.2 below to find out:

Figure 3.2 (Student Loan Comparison)

	Scenario 1	Scenario 2
Loan Amount	$29,400	$29,400
Interest Rate	6.8%	6.8%
Term of Loan	10 Years	20 Years
Monthly Payment	$338	$224
Total Amount Paid	$40,600	$53,861

The only difference between scenario A and B is the length of the term of the loan. In scenario A, the loan is paid back over 10 years. Scenario B pays back the loan in 20 years. While Scenario B may look more appealing due to a lower monthly payment, you'll end up paying over $13,000 more in interest costs over the life of the loan.

Regardless of the terms of the loan, you'll be obligated to make monthly payments for several years until it is paid off. While the above loan payments may seem reasonable, how do they fit in with your other expenses? When taken together with your other obligations, rent, food, transportation, etc. will you earn enough to cover everything? We specifically address this in Chapter 4 (Your Personal Finances).

Step 8 - Can you afford not to go?

While student loans provide a cautionary tale regarding the burdens of debt, it must be balanced against the opportunities of continuing your education. Ask yourself the following questions?

- ➤ Can you reach your goals if you don't go to school?
- ➤ Will you be able to earn what you deserve if you don't further your education?

If the answer to these questions is no, then determine the most cost effective path to reach your goals.

Informal Learning

When we think of learning, we often associate it within the context of a formal classroom setting. This is understandable as a majority of our first 18 years are spent in some type of formal education program. As noted earlier, decisions regarding what, when and where you learn were dictated by others. Your control over the situation was minimal at best.

> **Did you know?**
> More than 80% of learning is through informal means, and less than 20% through formal instruction.
> Source: The imperative-and the problems. By Robert S. Weintraub and Jennifer W. Martineau.

Informal learning, on the other hand, places the responsibility on your shoulders. It requires you to be proactive, take responsibility and seek out opportunities for self-improvement. Or, as Denis Waitley famously said, "View life as a continuous learning experience."

While it may not get the attention of formal learning, its impact can be far-reaching and have a profound impact on your life, both professionally and personally. This section looks at reasons for pursuing and the processes that will allow you to take full advantage of these opportunities.

Your Education

The Reasons

Your Career Depends On It

Companies operate in an environment of turbulent change. They are constantly under pressure to adapt to a shifting landscape of technology, societal changes, and global competition. To remain competitive in this dynamic environment, great companies know they must attract and retain the best and brightest employees. They know the best employees will help the company adapt, change, and thrive in this competitive landscape. While a business has to continually adjust to changing conditions, have you? Your ability to earn a paycheck depends on it. Your ability to earn a larger paycheck requires it. You must constantly improve your skill sets to remain relevant and valuable in the workplace.

Boredom (Your Career Depends On It - part II)

If you are employed, does it seem like your job is on autopilot? Do you do the same procedures and tasks all day and every day? You are there physically but not really mentally. This is career stagnation, an easy trap to fall into, and dangerous to your future employability. While you may be able to maintain your current job indefinitely, your skills slowly become less relevant. It can be hard to realize when this is happening and even harder to take action, but you must. Ask yourself, "Do my skills allow me to easily work for another employer, or are they only relevant at my current job?" If the answer is yes, you may need training and/or additional classes to help make your skill sets relevant to the larger marketplace.

Your Personality Depends On It

As noted above, it can be easy to get bored with your professional life. It can be just as easy to get into a rut regarding your personal life. Spending too much time looking at social media sites? Surfing the web on your phone? Watching TV? Outside of knowing the local gossip or what's happening on a TV drama show, do these types of behaviors make you interesting or different? Dare to be different and stretch your mind by learning something new. Having broader interests will help:

- Expand your social networks.
- Hone your conversational skills.
- Make you more interesting to your friends and co-workers.

Good social skills are closely tied to career growth and become increasingly important as your career matures.

Increases Confidence

Mastering a new skill, learning a new concept, or becoming more informed about a topic, works wonders for self-esteem and often sets the stage for personal growth. These types of activities challenge the status quo and require you to surmount a variety of obstacles. Your personal reward is the satisfaction of accomplishing something new and growing as a person.

Helps Keep You Relevant

Keeping in touch with the world, life's changing landscape, requires you to keep abreast of events that happen locally, nationally and worldwide. This demands an effort on your part to remain informed and up to date on a variety of issues. By doing this, you will become conversant on a wide range of topics and events. As noted before, human relation skills are valued over technical skills when moving into the higher levels of upper management.

The Process

Change requires altering your present behaviors in order to modify your future actions. It also requires a commitment to reach certain objectives at a certain time in the future. Dr. Phil articulated it more clearly when he said, "A goal without a deadline is just a dream." To be successful in this endeavor involves:

- Recording your behaviors over a specified period.
- Analyzing this information for any patterns.
- Removing those activities that keep you from reaching your goals.

Your Education

To begin the process, we recommend using a system that allows you to easily track your time. Use a method that feels comfortable but more importantly one that you will use. Some options are:

1. **Pencil and paper** - Write down your activities and the amount of time spent on each action during the day. Repeat each day for at least a week.

2. **Spreadsheet** – Use a pre-printed form like the one shown in Figure 3.3. This template can be downloaded at:

   http://calendar.wincalendar.net/Schedule_Templates/Schedule_Weekly_24_Hours.xls

   and allows you to record your activities in 15 minute increments, 24 hours a day for each day of the week.

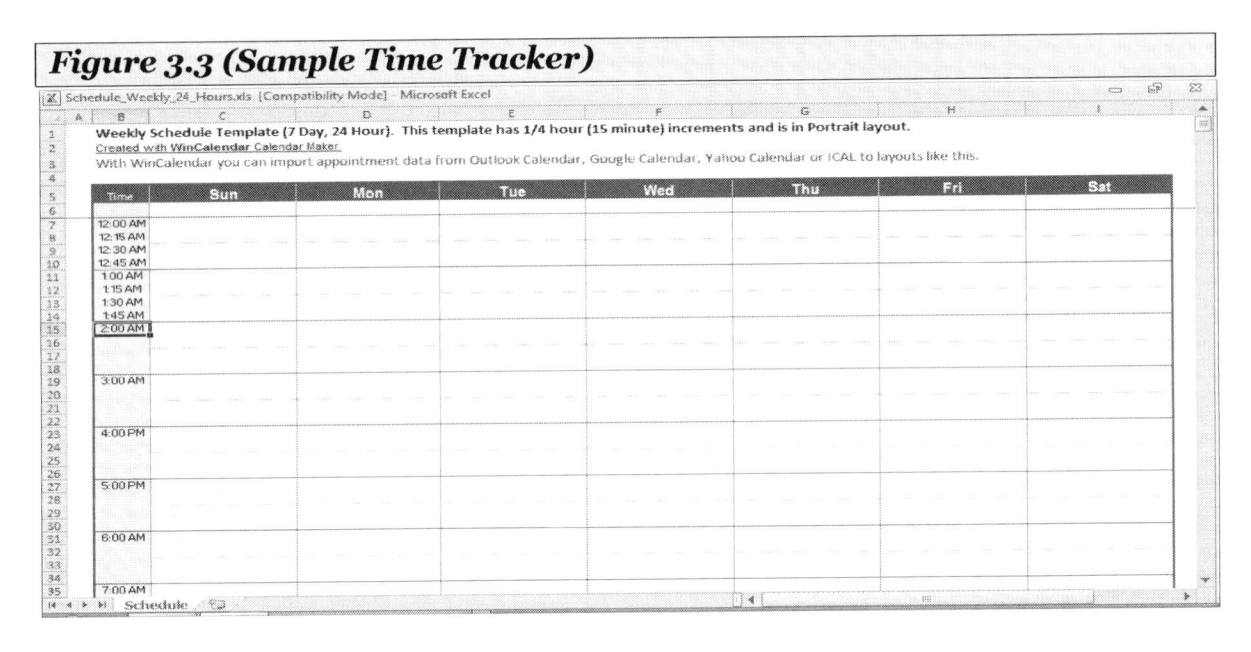

Figure 3.3 (Sample Time Tracker)

3. **App** - Technology has made the process of data collection easier than ever by allowing you to record your information on a tablet or smartphone. An example is shown in Figure 3.4.

- Google has a free version that can be accessed at:

  https://play.google.com/store/apps/details?id=com.dynamicg.timerecording&hl=en

- Apple also has an app that can be accessed for a small fee at:

  https://itunes.apple.com/us/app/eternity-time-log-personal/id296683442?mt=8

Figure 3.4 (Mobile Time Tracker App)

Regardless of the method used to collect your data, record all your daily activities for at least a week or longer, if possible. The more days tracked, the better you'll be able to see patterns in your behavior. You may be surprised by how much of your time is devoted to certain activities like TV, social media, surfing the Internet, and playing video games. Most, if not all, these types of behaviors do not actively challenge your intelligence. Ask yourself if these activities:

- Enrich my life?
- Make me a better person?
- Help me learn new things?

If you answered no to some or all of these, you may want to consider minimizing or replacing those activities with others that benefit you in some way. We now look at some of the ways to increase your knowledge both professionally and personally.

Professionally

Know your work

If you are currently working, do you know your job inside and out? Do you know the responsibilities of your co-workers? Are you aware of all the products your company makes and sells? Who are their competitors? If you do not know the answers to some or all of these, educate yourself on the environment in which you work.

Knowing everything about your job and the company increases your conceptual skills and better allows you to see the big picture (how everything is related). You will then be in a much better position to determine if your job can be done more efficiently and effectively. The process of educating yourself, analyzing your surroundings, and making thoughtful changes is a skill employers want, demand, and pay highly for. It:

1. Reflects a commitment to learning.
2. Allows you to become invaluable to the company.
3. Increases your knowledge and skill sets.
4. Will fill up your resume with action-related items that benefitted the company rather than just listings of just job duties and responsibilities.

Employees are the greatest resource of a company. The best companies realize this and provide ample opportunities for continuing education and training. It has been well established that regular training is linked to higher employee productivity. If you have a job, ask about any training. If you are in the process of trying to find a job, inquire about training as well. It can be a good indicator of whether or not an employer values its employees.

Training translates into more money in your pocket and increases your knowledge, value, and relevancy in the marketplace. There are a variety of ways to take advantage of learning opportunities at work such as:

Co-workers

As noted previously, approximately 80% of learning is through informal means. That means your fellow employees may be responsible for a significant portion of what you learn on the job. This places a great deal of responsibility on everyone in making sure everything is done correctly. The effects on your career can be positive and profound if your colleagues are enthusiastic, well-trained and follow the established rules. Or, they can be disruptive to your career if the conditions at work allow negativity, apathy, and little regard for rules and procedures. Therefore, pay attention and learn from those you work with that are the best and brightest. Your future depends upon it.

Mentoring

Mentoring takes place, either formally or informally, at work with a seasoned employee paired with someone new or less experienced. An effective way to transfer job knowledge, it is a way of providing assistance and support to new and less experienced employees. Take advantage of these opportunities by seeking out those considered experts at your company. Their expertise likely extends far beyond their job description and can provide a wealth of information regarding company policy and industry trends to name just a few. Because these individuals will likely have an extensive network of professionals, make it a point to get introduced to their contacts so you can begin building your own network of professionals.

Lunch and Learn

Many companies have employees that are experts in a wide array of topics. To take advantage of this knowledge, lunchtime can be turned into an informal way to learn about a variety of topics. This is a great way to tap internal resources and educate the workforce by teaching:

- Skills training
- Professional development
- Product training
- Sales training

If your company does not currently have a lunch and learn program, make a suggestion to your supervisor.

Conferences/Seminars/Lectures

Provide a valuable way to learn more about the other people and companies in your industry. While conferences often get a bad rap for being an inefficient use of time, they can provide a wealth of information regarding industry standards and best practices. Aside from important knowledge gained at these events, they also provide a chance for you to network with others outside your company. These relationships can be extremely important to your career and may provide a gateway to future job opportunities.

Know your resources

Are you using technology to your advantage at work? Do you know the ins and outs of the software programs you use on a regular basis? This is often one of the most underutilized company resources. Becoming an expert in these programs allows you to do your job more effectively and makes you valuable to current and future employers.

Obtain Certifications

Are there any certifications relevant to your career or industry? Along with expanding your knowledge base, they are a great way to increase job security and wages. Good employers encourage and even pay for certifications realizing that an educated workforce is productive and valuable.

Personally

Read

If you want to increase your knowledge, vocabulary, and ability to speak with persuasion, you must find time to read. Discover the time-wasters in your life by using the suggestions in the previous section. Use this extra time to read from a variety of sources such as books, blogs, magazines and newspapers. Read about what interests you but don't be afraid to venture into new topics and genres. Reading:

> **Did you know?**
> - 1/3 of high school graduates never read another book for the rest of their lives.
> - 42% of college graduates never read another book after college.
> - 80% of U.S. families did not buy or read a book last year
>
> Source: Jerold Jenkins
> www.JenkinsGroupInc.com

- Is an active process that makes you use your brain unlike passive activities such as television.
- Increases vocabulary and helps you use words more effectively when speaking.
- Builds self-esteem and allows you to become more knowledgeable about a variety of subject matters.
- Helps you become more conversant in a wider range of topics.

Having trouble finding the time or inclination to read on a consistent basis? Start or join a book club. Book clubs make you accountable to others, help you see different viewpoints, and provide practice speaking in front of a group. Another option is to download or rent the audio versions and listen to them while driving or doing a variety of other activities.

Take a class

Is there something that really interests you but you're not sure where to start? Adult education classes are a good place to begin and are often at convenient locations like the local library, community college, and adult education centers. Less formal than a college class, they provide a friendly environment with instructors who are passionate about the subject matter. If you can't find the topic or time to attend in person, check out the following on-line courses:

- Khan Academy http://www.khanacademy.org/
- Coursera https://www.coursera.org/
- Udacity https://www.udacity.com/
- MIT Open Courseware http://ocw.mit.edu/index.htm
- TEDed http://ed.ted.com/
- lynda.com http://www.lynda.com/

Join a Group

Either on-line or in person depending upon your interests, joining a group is a great way to stay motivated, meet new people, and experience new things.

Whether your goal is to ascend the corporate ladder, work for yourself, or just learn more about the world around you, lifelong learning is the key. Make continual learning a priority in your life and it will provide you with the skill sets to navigate the myriad of people and situations you will encounter in your journeys.

Chapter 4 – Your Personal Finances

"Before borrowing money from a friend, decide which you need most."
- American Proverb -

> **Did you know?**
> More than three-quarters of U.S. adults think they're good at managing their finances, but only 14% aced a 5-question quiz on basic financial concepts like interest rates, mortgages and inflation.
> Source: Investor Education Foundation of the Financial Industry Regulatory Authority (FINRA)

Finance is about keeping score. It's about tracking money earned and spent over a period of time (daily, weekly, bi-weekly, monthly, etc.). After everything has been added and subtracted, the results will yield either a surplus or a deficit. We will look more closely at this concept in a moment.

Obviously, everyone's (businesses and individuals) goal is to have a surplus. To help ensure that outcome, businesses closely track their finances on a daily/weekly/monthly basis in order to reach certain financial objectives. You must adopt this same behavior in order to reach your personal financial objectives. While the motives and operations of a business may differ significantly from your personal finances, the profit/savings objective is the same.

Throughout this book, we focus on business best practices to show how these same principles relate to your career. This chapter is no exception, and has particular relevance due to a growing proportion of individuals who struggle with financial literacy. In order to demystify the perceived complexities surrounding this issue, we look at those areas that will be of immediate benefit to you. Specifically, we:

- Define personal finance
- Discuss why credit matters
- See how much things really cost
- Look at the elements that make up your credit score
- Determine the Costs of Living

- Help you set up an organizing and tracking system
- Determine the best steps forward based on your situation

What is Personal Finance?

According to Wikipedia http://en.wikipedia.org/wiki/Personal_finance, "personal finance is the application of the principles of finance to the monetary decisions of an individual or family unit. It addresses the ways in which individuals or families obtain, budget, save, and spend monetary resources over time, taking into account various financial risks and future life events. Components of personal finance might include checking and savings accounts, credit cards and consumer loans, investments in the stock market, retirement plans, social security benefits, insurance policies, and income tax management."

That's the academic definition but probably not what people think when it comes to their finances. For most, it boils down to earning enough money to pay the bills. With luck, a little is left over at the end of the month to be used for any unexpected expenses. Sadly, many just barely squeak by or often spend more than they earn, further adding to a pile of debt that has been steadily accumulating.

To get a better perspective into personal finance, we look to the basic fundamental concept of any business. While passion may start a business, it is the selling of products and/or services at a profit that keeps it running. The word profit is underlined because without it, a business cannot survive. Profit is calculated by taking:

+ Revenue (income derived from selling products and services)

- Expenses (costs associated with making products and services)

= Profit/Loss

Assuming revenues are larger than expenses, a profit is earned. While this is always the goal of any business, sometimes expenses are greater than profits and a **loss** occurs. A company that continues to incur losses will eventually go out of business.

This same equation applies to you only it's worded a little differently:

- + **Revenue** (salary or wages received from your employer)
- − **Expenses** (costs associated with living, rent, food, clothing, etc.)
- = **Savings**/**Debt**

Assuming your wages are larger than your expenses, **savings** occurs. If the money you earn can't pay for all of your expenses, **debt** occurs. An individual that continues to incur debts will go bankrupt.

Although they differ in many respects, individuals and businesses still must operate under similar financial principles. They are:

- ➢ Act responsibly
- ➢ Live within your means
- ➢ Plan for the future
- ➢ Spend less than you make

The importance of these basic financial tenets, especially the last one, can greatly affect your personal and professional life as we shall see in the next section.

Why Credit Matters

Before discussing budgets, savings, checking accounts, spending, and all the other areas associated with your finances, we need to find out what others (financial institutions) think about your current financial standing. Prior to lending, financial institutions obtain information about your creditworthiness from the three big credit reporting agencies (Transunion, Equifax, and Experian). These ratings, discussed more in-depth later in this chapter, are used to determine the risk associated with loaning you money. They affect you in the following ways:

1. **Access to Credit** - A favorable credit rating (good credit score) allows easier access to loans, credit cards and other types of financing. Conversely, an unfavorable credit rating (low credit score) hinders access to borrowing.

2. **Costs** – The cost of financing is directly related to your credit history. Borrowers with good credit scores:

    - Are considered a low risk for default.
    - Are charged lower interest rates.
    - Pay less interest costs on loans.

   The reverse is true for borrowers with bad credit scores and often means hundreds, if not thousands, more in borrowing costs due to perceived credit risks by the lender.

3. **Employability** - The third, and perhaps most important area, involves employee suitability. Before making hiring decisions, employers use a variety of methods to find out more about a candidate. Background checks, including credit history, are increasingly being used to show patterns of behavior that may affect the employer/employee relationship. Employers note that poor credit scores raise concerns regarding a candidate's honesty and integrity and may be a predictor of future performance.

Increasingly stringent hiring practices are resulting in many more candidates being rejected in the hiring process due to poor credit ratings. According to a 2012 study by the Society of Human Resources Management, 47% of companies conduct pre-employment credit checks on some candidates and 13% conduct them on all candidates. This is a trend that will continue, as employers try to minimize the risks of hiring unsuitable candidates that could harm the company or its clients.

Don't let this type of information derail your job search or career. Take a proactive approach and know your credit rating. A free report can be requested once a year at the following:

> **Did you know?**
> 22% of Americans say that they have never taken the time to order a copy of their credit reports, despite the fact that consumers can order them free of charge under federal laws.
> Source: www.FindLaw

http://www.ftc.gov/bcp/edu/pubs/consumer/credit/cre34.shtm

Checking your credit report on annual basis allows you to:

- Verify that the information is accurate and up-to-date.
- Explain any irregularities that may have compromised your finances such as unplanned medical expenses, divorce, etc.

➢ Guard against fraud and identity theft.

If your credit report looks okay, it should not hinder you in the job search process. If you feel there are any errors or discrepancies on your report, get them fixed as soon as possible by going to the following:
http://www.myfico.com/CreditEducation/Questions/Error-On-Credit-Report.aspx

Consider your credit report your financial resume and treat it with the same care and reverence as your regular resume. The good news is that 65% of companies SHRM surveyed give candidates the opportunity to explain their credit history. Employers don't like surprises. Get out ahead of any bad news by explaining your situation. Steer the focus back to the value you can bring to the company. If necessary, ask for a six-month probationary period to allow you adequate time to address the issues on your credit report.

Financing - What Do Things Really Cost?

In the previous section, we discussed the importance of requesting your credit report, reading the material thoroughly, and verifying all the information contained within. We now look at how this information (a record of your past behaviors) affects the costs of future purchases. Specifically, we will focus on the financing costs associated with purchasing a car and a house.

Our first example, Figure 4.1, shows the cost of purchasing a $20,000 car under three different credit rating scenarios (good credit, poor credit, and very poor credit).

Figure 4.1 (Car Loan)

Credit Rating	Good	Poor	Very Poor
Loan Amount	$20,000	$20,000	$20,000
Interest Rate	5%	7%	10%
Loan Term	60 Months (5 yrs)	60 Months (5 yrs)	60 Months (5 yrs)
Monthly Payment	377.42	396.02	424.94
Total Interest Paid	2,645.48	3,761.44	5,496.40
Total Amount Paid (Principal and Interest)	$22,645.48	$23,761.44	$25,496.40

Credit ratings directly affect the loans issued by financial institutions and the differences can be quite pronounced. A person with a good credit rating is viewed as low risk, likely to pay back the loan in a timely manner, and subsequently is given favorable loan terms (lower interest rates). Conversely, a person with a very poor credit rating is viewed as high risk, less likely to pay the loan back in a timely manner, and is subsequently given less than favorable loan terms (higher interest rates). The higher the interest rate, the costlier the loan.

The difference in monthly payments between the person with good credit and very poor credit is almost $70 per month. While that may not seem like much, over the life of the loan it adds up to more than $2,800 in interest charges. Multiply that by the number of cars you may own in a lifetime, and it could add up to tens of thousands of dollars.

We now do the same exercise, but use the purchase of a $150,000 house as our example. Details are shown in Figure 4.2 below.

Figure 4.2 (House Loan)

Credit Rating	Good	Poor	Very Poor
Loan Amount	$150,000	$150,000	$150,000
Interest Rate	5%	7%	10%
Loan Term	360 mo. (30 yrs)	360 mo. (30 yrs)	360 mo. (30 yrs)
Monthly Payment	$805.23	$997.95	$1,316.36
Total Interest Paid	$139,883.68	$209,263.35	$323,888.65
Total Amount Paid (Principal and Interest)	$289,883.68	$359,263.35	$473,888.65

Again, we highlight the differences between someone with a good credit rating and someone with a very bad credit rating. The difference in monthly payments is a little over $500, or more than $6,000 per year. It gets worse when we look at the interest paid over the lifetime of the loan. That difference works out to be approximately $184,000 over the life of the loan. Finally, the discrepancy in what our two borrowers pay back to the mortgage company in principal and interest is staggering. The person with a good credit rating pays a total loan amount of $289,883.68 for a $150,000 loan while the person with a very poor credit rating ends up paying $473,888.65 for the same loan. That is almost three times the value of the original loan amount of $150,000.

As you can see poor credit makes everything more expensive and is not just limited to larger purchases you'll make in life. Other organizations, such as mobile phone companies, insurance companies, landlords, and government departments use this information in deciding if they want to do business with you. Because this information is so pervasive and easily obtainable, we recommend checking and verifying your credit history as soon as possible.

What Is Your Credit Score?

While the previous sections of this chapter have noted the pitfalls of bad credit, we now focus on the information contained in your report and the role it plays in calculating your credit score. This score is derived from your credit report and translated into a number that represents your creditworthiness. Your number will fall into one of the ranges listed below in Figure 4.3.

Note: *Credit report disclosures do not include credit scores. Your credit score disclosure must be purchased separately. However, you can request to purchase your credit score disclosure when you request your free annual credit file disclosure.*

Figure 4.3 (Credit Scoring Table)

Credit Range	Credit Rating
Between 700 and 850	Very good or excellent
Between 680 and 699	Good credit
Between 620 and 679	Average or OK
Between 580 and 619	Low credit
Between 500 and 579	Poor credit
Between 300 and 499	Bad credit

The above information was obtained from http://creditscoresrange.net/.

Read over the information contained in your report and contact each lending institution to correct any inaccuracies and make necessary corrections. It is crucial that this information be as accurate as possible because of its impact on your credit score.

Below we look at the five factors used to calculate your credit score:

1. **Payment History** – What better way to judge someone than by looking at their past performance. A good part of your score is a reflection of how well you have paid your debts over time. A missed payment or two can be the difference between an average score and a great score. From now on, try and make all payments in a timely fashion and watch your score go up.

2. **Amount Borrowed** - Carry around many credit cards? That's ok! It's not the number of cards that you have but the balances on each. Using 50% or more of your available credit will have a negative impact on your score. This is a warning sign to lenders that you may have trouble meeting your debt obligations in the future. Better to have many cards with small balances than one or a few that are maxed out.

3. **Credit History** - The general rule is the longer your history of making payments the better. Statistics show that people with exceptional credit scores have on average 3 credit cards that have been open seven years or longer. If you pay off your balances, you may want to keep the cards open. If you have many cards and don't want the accounts any longer, close them over a period of time to lessen the impact on your credit score.

4. **Applications for Credit** – Numerous inquiries into your credit history can adversely affect your score.

5. **Credit Mix** - Having different types of debt (home loan, car loan, student loan, credit card, business loan, etc.) and the ability to successfully manage these loans will have a positive impact on your score.

Experian, one of the big three credit reporting bureaus, states in its marketing materials, "Credit information provides insight into an applicant's integrity and responsibility toward his or her financial obligations." Most businesses use credit checks only to screen for certain positions, but one in eight, the survey found, does a credit check before every hire.

Look at what some of the experts say:

- "Credit is one data point that businesses are using to get an overall feel," Mr. Clemans said. "Does this consumer have a lifestyle that fits the job? Is this someone who I can trust?" It is not the only factor, said Terry W. Clemans, executive director of the National Consumer Reporting Association.

- The website of a pre-employment screening company, Info Cubic, says, "A credit report can be an important indicator of financial responsibility for employees with fiduciary or cash handling responsibilities, access to expensive equipment, other people's property, or otherwise placed in a position of financial trust."

- Experian's pitch is more ominous: "Every time you hire a new employee you put a lot on the line," says a company brochure. "The wrong decision could jeopardize your firm's assets, reputation, or security."

Because this is so important to your long-term financial health, how can you raise your score? George DeMare, Managing Partner of Midwest Mortgage Capital, says two things have the greatest impact. "Pay your bills on time, and borrowing sparingly. That is the best way to fix credit over time."

Because your financial history is used to make assumptions about your future behavior, take time to review your credit report, know your score, and take steps to correct any mistakes.

The Costs of Living

Whether you know it or not, you are running a business and that business is life. That means earning enough money to cover the basic necessities of food, clothing, and housing. To be successful at this endeavor, you'll need to keep score by tracking your earnings (revenue) and spending (expenses).

While the majority of this book focuses on increasing the revenue side of the equation, this chapter's focus is about expenses and making better financial decisions. In this section, we specifically focus on the various costs associated with day-to-day living. We start by looking at one of the largest but most often overlooked expenses that occur throughout your lifetime, taxes. Next, we examine common expenditures you'll likely incur such as housing, food, clothing, etc. Finally, we show how this all fits together by constructing a sample personal income and expense (pie) statement.

Expenses -Taxes

Before any money ever reaches your hand, it has usually been taxed in some way. The money you earn at work is no exception. Periodically, usually every 1 to 2 weeks, your employer will issue you a paycheck. Attached to your paycheck is the calculation of your pay for the period in question. In simple terms, it shows:

+ **Gross wages (revenue)**
- **Various taxes (expenses)**
- <u>**Other withholdings**</u>
= **Net Pay**

For our purposes, and for the sake of simplicity, we will focus just on the taxes that are most commonly withheld by an employer. These withheld taxes are then sent to various government agencies (federal, state, local) by the employer on your behalf and credited against any money you may owe at the end of the year. A final reconciliation takes place when you file your taxes. If you paid more taxes than required, you'll be entitled to a refund. If you paid less tax than required, you'll have to make up the difference when you file your tax returns. The types of taxes withheld from your paycheck are:

Federal Taxes - Abbreviated as Fed Tax, FT, or FWT

The amount withheld depends on:

- If you are married or single.

- The number of allowances you indicated on Form W-4 that you filed with your employer when you first started. You can claim a withholding allowance:

  - For yourself unless someone else (spouse or parent) lists you as a dependent on their tax return.

- ❖ For your spouse unless they already claimed an allowance at their work.
- ❖ For each of your children unless they have already been claimed by a spouse.

The amount of federal taxes withheld depends upon the number of allowances you claim. The more dependents you claim, the less taxes will be withheld from your paycheck.

The rates of withholding vary depending on your filing status (single, married filing jointly, married filing separately, and head of household). For our purposes, and to simplify, we use the tables for a single payer and listed below in Figure 4.4.

Figure 4.4 (2013 Withholding Tables - Single Filer)

If taxable income is more than ...	but not more than ...	the tax is ...
$0	$8,925	10% of the taxable income
$8,926	$36,250	$893 plus 15% of the amount over $8,926
$36,251	$87,850	$5,438 plus 25% of the amount over $36,251
$87,851	$183,250	$21,963 plus 28% of the amount over $87,851
$183,251	$398,350	$51,310 plus 33% of the amount over $183,251
$398,351	$400,000	$131,456 plus 35% of the amount over $398,351
$400,000	N/A	$140,000 plus 39.6% of the amount over $400,000

Figure 4.4 lists the marginal tax rates in place for 2013. Marginal means you are taxed in steps rather than on just one flat rate. For example, suppose your earnings for the year were $50,000. Looking at the above table, $50,000 falls between the $36,251 and $87,850 range. The federal tax you would owe at the end of the year would be:

$5,438 (as noted from row 3, column 3 of Figure 4.4)
+$3,437 = 25% x (50,000 - 36,251)
$8,875 = Amount of federal taxes you would owe for the year

Your tax rate would be 17.75% = $8,875/$50,000. This is the marginal, or blended, rate and is a combination of the rates (10%, 15%, and 25%) listed in the first three lines of Figure 4.4 above.

Earning $50,000 per year really means you take home only $41,125 after federal taxes are withheld. On a weekly basis, this equals:

$961.54 Weekly pay ($50,000/52)
- $170.67 Federal taxes ($8,875/52)
$790.87 Net pay after federal taxes withheld

Before receiving any money from your paycheck, your earnings are reduced by approximately 18% in federal taxes as shown above. Withholdings for other payroll taxes (state, local, etc.) will also be withheld from your paycheck, are discussed below, and further decrease your pay. Therefore, take the time to manually calculate what is being withdrawn from your paycheck to ensure accuracy. Let's look at the other taxes that may be withheld from your pay.

State Taxes - Abbreviated as St Tax, ST, or SWT

Unlike federal taxes, the state you live in determines the amount of taxes withheld from your paycheck, if any. This rate will vary and can be found at:

http://www.taxadmin.org/fta/rate/tax_stru.html

Local Taxes - Abbreviated as LT, LST

Local taxes are withheld by the jurisdiction (county, city, township, borough, etc.) to help pay for services provided in the area in which you live and/or work. Typically, these taxes are levied by city or county governments and school districts. The name of all taxing jurisdictions will be listed on your paystub.

(OASDI) Old-Age, Survivors, and Disability Insurance or more commonly known as Social Security - Abbreviated as FICA, SS, SSWT, or OASDI*

The rate of withholding is 6.2% of your total pay up to a certain income level. For 2013, the level was $113,700. Your employer is required to match that amount but it doesn't come out of your pay.

Medicare - Abbreviated as MWT or Med*

The Medicare withholding rate is 1.45% of all income. Unlike social security, there are no income limits. Therefore all wages are subject to the Medicare tax. Also, beginning in 2013 you must pay 0.9% more in Medicare taxes on earned individual income of more than $200,000. Like social security, your employer matches the amount you contribute but it doesn't come out of your pay.

* Unlike the other taxes listed above, Social Security and Medicare withholdings are collected in the present in order to provide you with future medical care (Medicare) and retirement benefits (Social Security).

Miscellaneous Withholdings

Other items that may be withheld from your paycheck are:

- **Health Insurance Premiums** - Your employer may provide health insurance coverage for you and your dependents. However, you may be asked to pay for some or all of the premiums.
- **Life Insurance Premiums** - Your employer may purchase a life insurance policy on your behalf. You may be asked to pay for some or all

of the premiums for the policy. In many cases, the employer will pay for 100% of the premiums on a policy that is equal to your yearly salary. If you want to increase the coverage amounts, you'll be asked to pay for the increase in premiums associated with the increased policy coverage.

- ➢ **Retirement Plans** - You may have the chance to contribute a percentage of your salary to a 401(k), 403(b), or other type of plan that defer your income in the present to be used as income in the future (retirement). Your pay stub will reflect the amount and type of these contributions. We encourage you to take advantage of this benefit, if possible, as it helps set aside money for your retirement. Just as important, any amounts you contribute may reduce your taxable income for the year.

- ➢ **Section 125 Plans (Cafeteria Plans)** - Many employers maintain these types of plans to allow employees a chance to defer part of their salary to pay for expenses like health insurance, child care, adoption services, etc. These plans allow you to pay for expenses using money before it has been taxed.

Ask your employer for information and clarification regarding any of the above-mentioned items

We have analyzed the taxes withheld from your paycheck because they are one of the first expenses you will incur when employed. They can take away a significant portion of your earnings and reduce the amount of money available for other costs associated with your life.

While it is our civic duty to pay taxes, it is also important for you to know just how much you are paying and to reduce these expenses where possible. While you cannot control the amount you pay for most of the items listed above, a few of them are determined by where you live and work (state and local taxes). If possible, try and live and work in those jurisdictions that levy a lower tax rate than their neighbor states. While the differences may seem small, these taxes can really add up over several years.

At the end of the year, your employer is required to provide you with Form W-2. This is a federal tax form providing a summation of what you were paid during the year along with any taxes or items withheld from your paycheck. It is a good idea to compare your last pay stub for the year with the W-4. The year-to-date totals on your last pay stub for the year should equal the totals listed on your W-4. If they do not match, contact your employer to see where any discrepancies may have occurred.

Expenses - Needs (Non-Discretionary Spending)

We now turn our attention to the major expenses associated with your day-to-day activities. These are the needs in life and are non-discretionary (must be purchased) expenses to ensure your survival. For our purposes, we'll concentrate on housing, transportation, food, health insurance, clothing, and personal care. While these can vary widely from person to person, we'll use information compiled from the federal government where possible in order to be as consistent and accurate as possible. Specifically, we utilized information from http://www.bls.gov/cex/csxann11.pdf for some of the categories discussed below:

Housing

Rent or mortgage payments will often be the largest monthly expense in your budget. Because of this, we look more closely at:

- The major reasons for renting.
- The major reasons for buying.
- The expenses associated with renting and buying.
- Location and its effect on costs.

Finally, we'll determine an appropriate monthly housing cost to be used for our sample personal income and expense (pie) worksheet.

Why Rent?

- The landlord is responsible for any maintenance issues.
- Uncertainty in your employment or income provides the flexibility to quickly move, if necessary.
- Small upfront costs (first month's rent along with a possible security deposit).
- Helps you establish a credit history.
- Purchasing a house requires a much larger outlay of funds initially and usually on an ongoing basis.

Why Buy?

- Paying rent goes to the landlord with nothing to show at the end of the month.
- Each mortgage payment increases your ownership in your home.
- You can deduct certain expenses associated with a home on your taxes.
- You have greater control over the living space and can make alterations to the dwelling that range from cosmetic to major structural changes.

Regardless of your choice of living arrangements, make sure this expense is not so large that you have difficulty making ends meet. A good rule to follow is that rent or mortgage payments should not exceed 25% of your monthly income. For example, if you make $30,000 per year, $2,500/month, your rent or mortgage payment should be no more than $625 per month.

Expense Comparisons

Figure 4.5 below shows an overview of the type of housing expenses you'll encounter when renting or buying. A "Y" indicates a monthly expense associated with a particular category while an "N" means that it is not applicable. Before renting or buying, takes these into consideration as they can have a significant impact on your budget.

Figure 4.5 (Housing Expense Items)

Expense	Heating/ Cooling	Water/ Sewer	Trash	Property Taxes	Homeowner's Insurance	Rental Insurance	Maintenance	Cleaning Supplies
Renting	Y	Y	Y	N	N	Y	N	Y
Buying	Y	Y	Y	Y	Y	N	Y	Y

Heating/Cooling

Involves the purchase of utilities such as electricity, natural gas, propane, or some combination of both in order to heat or cool your living spaces. These expenses may be small or large depending on where you live, how big your living space is, the time of year, and fluctuations in price due to market conditions.

Water/Sewer

A clean water source, as well as proper sewage removal, is part of the basic necessities required for every dwelling. If renting, these utilities may or may not be included as part of the rent you pay each month. If buying, you will likely pay these expenses directly to a local municipality based on usage or in the form of taxes.

Trash

Most, if not all, apartments have a common area where renters can deposit their trash. While each renter may be billed directly for this service, it is often included as part of your rental payment. Homeowners, on the other hand, have to purchase these services directly from a local refuse company. Rates and types of services will vary depending upon the plan chosen.

If you are a renter, the three items mentioned above may be billed to you directly or included in the rent you pay each month. This is why the price of rent can vary dramatically from one place to the next. If these are included in your rent, your landlord has previously determined what these expenses will be and passed the costs along to you. If they are not included in your rent, you will be billed directly from each provider. Take this into account when comparing rental prices so you can make an informed financial decision.

Know your expenses before renting or buying by figuring out what a good estimate of what these costs will be. If you are going to rent, the rental agent should be able to provide a good approximation of what your costs will be. If you are buying a house, ask the home seller for the approximate costs they incurred regarding utility bills over the preceding 12 months. This proactive approach will help you avoid surprises at the end of the month and further allow you to refine your budget.

Property Taxes

While they can go by different names (real estate, property or millage) these are taxes imposed on the value of your house and any other real estate holdings you own. These taxes are paid by homeowners to the local school district in which they reside and help fund the operations of the public schools. The following link http://interactive.taxfoundation.org/propertytax/ allows you to see the median rates paid in your area for past years.

Depending upon the value of the house, the yearly bill for these taxes can be substantial. Do your research and know what these expenses are before purchasing a home. Do you know that renters also pay property taxes, albeit indirectly? The person(s) or company that you rent from pays property taxes. These taxes, like the other items listed above (heating/cooling, water/sewer, and trash) are often paid by the landlord. The landlord then passes them along to you in the form of higher rent.

Homeowners Insurance

While not required, it is important to insure your home against any kind of damage that may occur. From the website www.homeinsurance.com the national average rate of homeowners insurance was $900. This figure can vary a great deal depending upon where you live and the assessed value of the property.

Rental Insurance

Although it is not a requirement, it is highly recommended that you purchase this type of insurance. Per State Farm Insurance Company, "The average person has over $20,000 worth of belongings that are probably not covered by a landlord's policy." Cost of coverage is normally in the range of $10 - $25 per month and would provide coverage for your possessions. It also offers protection if someone is injured at your place and sues you. Your legal expenses and court settlement could be covered by your policy. At the risk of losing all your belongings, paying an extra $150 - $300 per year is well worth it

Maintenance

All houses require upkeep, some more than others, and depends largely on the age and condition of the house. Because this amount can vary greatly, it is difficult to pinpoint an average yearly cost. However, keep this in mind when purchasing a house by setting aside money for unplanned and unforeseen events. As noted in the chart above, maintenance expenses are not applicable to renters because the landlord is responsible for any issues regarding your living space.

Housekeeping and Supplies

Defined by the IRS as, "Housekeeping supplies include laundry and cleaning supplies, stationery supplies, postage, delivery services, miscellaneous household products, and lawn and garden supplies." Again, these will vary per person and type of housing (renting versus buying).

Where to Live?

A big part of your housing cost is determined by where you choose to live. A similar house or apartment can be more or less expensive depending on the location you choose and can easily result in a difference of several hundred dollars per month. Before settling on a place, research the neighborhood regarding rental rates/house prices, local tax rates, crime statistics, and the public schools. Schools are a great indicator of the type of people and businesses in a particular area. A great place to find this information is on-line. However, there is nothing like first-hand information gained from friends, family, and current residents. Your research should allow you to get a feel for what is available and within your price range.

Housing Costs

Because housing expenses are unique for each person, it can be difficult to estimate this monthly cost. For help, we turned to the U.S. Bureau of Labor Statistics. Based on the consumer expenditures for 2011, the yearly cost associated with housing was $16,803 for one consumer unit. A consumer unit is defined as 2.5 people. This means that the housing cost for one person per month is $560 = $16,803/12 months/2.5. This figure includes any payments made for rent/mortgage, utilities, operations, supplies, furnishings, and equipment. We'll use the monthly amount calculated above for our "pie" statement at the end of this chapter.

Transportation

For many, having a car is not an option and often the only viable means of getting from point A to point B. This is especially true if you live in a suburban or rural environment. Because it's a necessity, and can be one of the biggest monthly expenses outside of housing costs, your goal should be to minimize your outlay where possible. Below we look at the expenses you will likely incur on a monthly basis.

Car Purchase

The type of car you buy, and more importantly its price, will determine your monthly payment obligation. In a perfect world, paying cash and not having to borrow is the ideal situation. Unfortunately this is usually not an option for most. Therefore, choosing the most affordable and practical vehicle goes a long way toward minimizing these costs and keeping within your budget. A great way to reduce your expenses is to buy a used car instead of a new one. This difference is highlighted below in Figure 4.6. Vehicle A is used and priced at $10,000 and vehicle B is new and priced at $20,000. The terms of the loan are equal in all other aspects.

Figure 4.6 - Vehicle Purchase (Used vs. New)					
Vehicle	Purchase Price	Interest Rate	Term of Loan	Monthly Payment	Total Payments
A (Used)	$10,000	5%	60 Months	$189	$11,323
B (New)	$20,000	5%	60 Months	$377	$22,646

As you can see, the purchase price ($10,000 vs. $20,000) and monthly payment ($189 vs. $377) between Vehicle A and Vehicle B are significant. If the entire purchase price of each vehicle is financed, Vehicle B will end up costing over $11,000 more than Vehicle A ($11,323 vs. $22,646). That is a substantial amount of money and can have quite an impact on your budget. Therefore, proceed cautiously when making these types of large purchases by knowing all your options.

Fuel

Normally, the emphasis on buying a car is the purchase price and rightly so due to the effect it can have on your monthly budget. However, the next biggest expense in car ownership is fuel costs. Because there are large differences in fuel mileage among cars, it should play a part in your decision-making process. To see how much it can affect your budget, we compare the monthly costs of two vehicles in Figure 4.7. Vehicle A gets 20 miles to the gallon (MPG) and Vehicle B gets 35 MPG.

Figure 4.7 - Fuel Cost Comparison

Vehicle	Miles/Gallon (MPG)	Price/Gallon	Miles Driven Per Year	Monthly Costs	Yearly Costs	5 Year Costs
A	20	$3.25	15,000	$203	$2,438	$12,190
B	35	$3.25	15,000	$116	$1,393	$6,964
Difference				$87	$1,045	$5,226

The cost differences are apparent after the first month, with the owner of Vehicle A spending $87 more per month on fuel than the owner of Vehicle B. That equates to $87 more in your pocket each and every month and more than $5,000 over a five-year period.

To help you make a more informed decision, automakers provide a great deal of information on the window sticker of each car. According to www.cars.com, "The window sticker, known as a Monroney label, must include a more comprehensive fuel economy and environment section. This includes information about fuel-cost estimates, emissions ratings, alternative-fuel vehicles, and additional efficiency details. To the right of the fuel-economy information is an estimate of how much money you will save on fuel costs over five years compared to the average new vehicle. Below that are estimated annual fuel costs as well as a fuel-economy and greenhouse-gas rating and a smog rating, both on a scale from one to 10, with 10 the best score." An example of what this information looks like is shown in Figure 4.8 below.

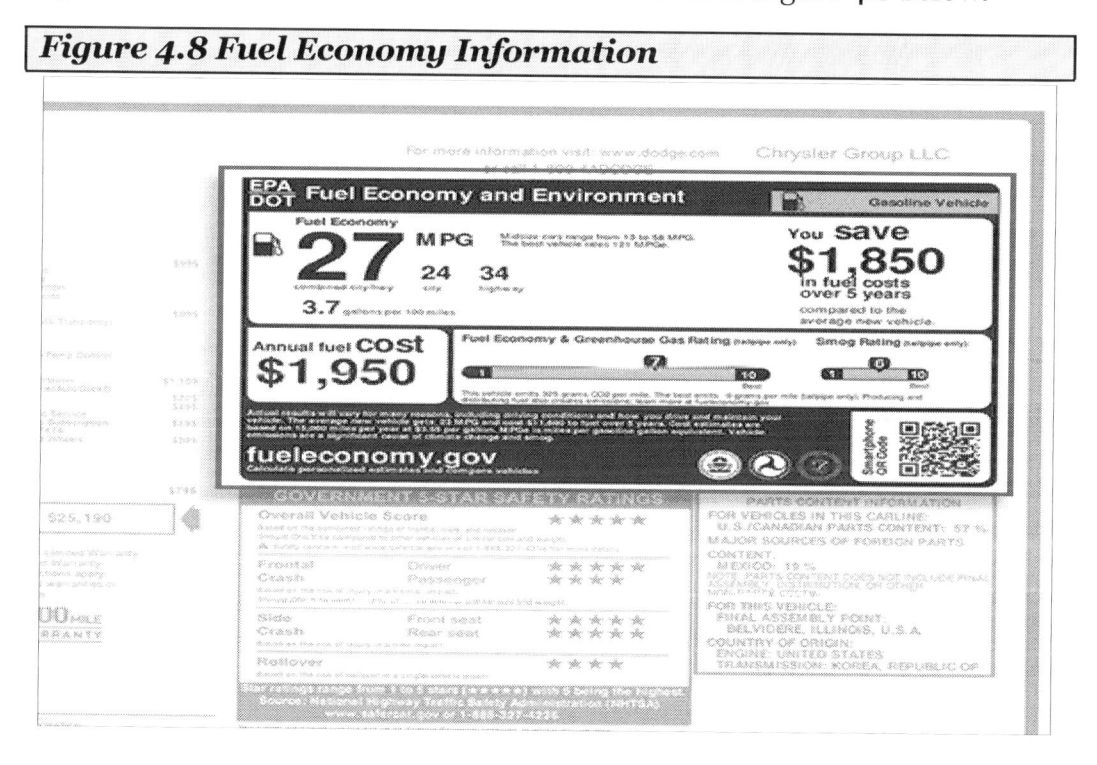

Figure 4.8 Fuel Economy Information

For used cars, information regarding the approximate mileage you can expect can be found at http://www.fueleconomy.gov/feg/findacar.shtml. If you want to compare the mileage of two different cars, use the following link: http://www.fueleconomy.gov/feg/savemoney.shtml.

Maintenance

Many consumers rarely consider the cost of vehicle maintenance when deciding on the type of car to purchase. Just like the price and mileage discussed above, vehicle maintenance will also have an impact on your budget. Edmonds www.edmonds.com recently looked at the maintenance costs for the top best selling cars. Figure 4.9 shows two cars with the highest and lowest costs per 75,000 miles driven. We assume that the average mileage driven for a year is 15,000 miles.

Figure 4.9 - Maintenance Costs

Vehicle	Monthly Cost	Yearly Cost	Five Year Cost
Toyota Camry	$14	$169	$2,028
Honda CR-V	$7	$81	$973
Difference	**$7**	**$88**	**$1,055**

The differences may seem insignificant or inconsequential in the present but slowly start to add up when taken together with all the others items in your budget.

Automobile Insurance

If you drive, automobile insurance is compulsory in every state except New Hampshire. Because this cost pertains to a significant portion of the population, we include it under our non-discretionary expenses. Car insurance is determined by many variables such as your age, where you live, type of vehicle, number of miles driven, your driving record, etc. Therefore, take the time to determine the best coverage for you at the best price. This means getting at least three quotes before purchasing. A survey of the average monthly auto insurance rates per state from www.insurancequotesusa.com yield a range from $46.17 to $98.67. For purposes of our sample budget, we'll take an average of these two numbers and use a rate of $72/month for automobile insurance.

True Cost to Own

Instead of searching many different places to find the information discussed above, Edmunds has made this process much easier with their True Cost to Own® (TCO) pricing website http://www.edmunds.com/tco.html. It notes the following, "The Edmunds Inc. True Cost to Own® (TCO) pricing system calculates the additional costs you may not have included when considering your next vehicle purchase. These extra costs include: depreciation, interest on your loan, taxes and fees, insurance premiums, fuel costs, maintenance, and repairs." Type in the make, model, year, and style of the car(s) you are interested in buying and it will calculate the total cost of ownership over a five-year period. This valuable information will help you make a more informed buying decision that has immediate and long term budget consequences.

Food

Food plays an essential role in our lives and can easily take up a significant portion of your budget. Depending on the size of a family, it can end up being one of your largest monthly expenses. Because this expense varies from person to person, we utilized the United States Department of Agriculture (USDA) website for help in determining these costs. Their website http://www.cnpp.usda.gov/USDAFoodCost-Home.htm provides an excellent breakdown of the average costs to feed a person each month.

For our budget, we used the calculations for a family of four (2 adults and 2 children) and divided this number by 4 to get an individual amount of:

Food Budget/Person $ 256/month*

* The above amount is for a family of four defined as a Couple 19-50 years of age and 2 children ages 6-8 and 9-11 under the moderate-cost plan level. Total monthly cost equals $1,023.10. Divided by 4 for an individual amount of $255.78. This information is from:

http://www.cnpp.usda.gov/Publications/FoodPlans/2012/CostofFoodNov2012.pdf

Health Insurance

Health insurance premiums continue to increase each year and the trend is likely to persist for the foreseeable future. Like other types of insurance, the amount paid in premiums are determined by the type of plan you choose and the risk factors you present to an insurance company. Prior to the Affordable Care Act, many risk factors were taken into account to determine what your monthly health insurance premium would be. These factors included your age, gender, current health, past health issues, pre-existing conditions, and if you smoke. The Affordable Care Act simplified this approach and now uses just two factors to determine your insurance premiums, how old you are and where you live.

While the cost of insurance varies from person to person, so does the payer of these premiums. Depending upon where you work, the employer may pay all, some, or none of your health care costs. This can easily be one of your largest monthly expenses. Therefore, it is very important to know the benefits, if any, provided by your employer. When comparing job offers, compare and contrast what each offers in terms of pay and benefits. While the pay from one company may be lower, its overall benefit package may actually be worth more than the company offering higher pay.

For our budget, we'll utilize the data compiled in the Kaiser Family Foundation's 2012 survey http://ehbs.kff.org/pdf/2012/8346.pdf. They indicate the average annual premiums for employer-sponsored health insurance are $5,884 for single coverage per year and $16,351 for family coverage per year. For our budget, we'll use the single rate and assume the employer pays at least 50% of the monthly premium. This works out to:

$$\text{Health Insurance Premium} = \$245/\text{month} \ (\$5,884/12/2)$$

Clothing & Apparel

In trying to determine a good average cost associated with this category, we sought the guidance from the following IRS publications.

> http://www.irs.gov/Businesses/Small-Businesses-&-Self-Employed/National-Standards-Food-Clothing-and-Other-Items

> http://www.irs.gov/pub/irs-utl/national_standards-2012.pdf

Their definition of this category states that "apparel and services includes clothing, footwear, material, patterns and notions for making clothes, alterations and repairs, clothing rental, clothing storage, dry cleaning and sent-out laundry, watches, jewelry and repairs to watches and jewelry." Using their assessment, the allowable living expense for one person is:

Apparel and Services = $86/month

Personal Care Products & Services

To be consistent, we will also use the IRS standards for Housekeeping Supplies and Personal Care Products & Services. These are defined by the IRS as, "Personal care products and services includes products for the hair, oral hygiene products, shaving needs, cosmetics and bath products, electric personal care appliances, and other personal care products." It amounts to:

Personal Care Products and Services = $32/month

Expenses - Wants (Discretionary Spending)

Per Investopedia, discretionary income is defined as "the amount of an individual's income that is left for spending, investing or saving after taxes and personal necessities (such as food, shelter, and clothing) have been paid. Discretionary income includes money spent on luxury items, vacations and non-essential goods and services."

This definition is highly relevant for our purposes because discretionary expenses often determine whether your budget is in the black (you made more than you spent during the month) or, your budget is in the red (you spent more money than you made during the month). An easy way to limit your expenses in the future is to ask yourself the following question: "Is this item I am about to purchase a want or a need? If it is a need, then it's probably a necessity and should be purchased. If it is a want, then it's probably not a necessity and does not need to be purchased.

The costs of living can add up very quickly as will be shown in the personal income and expense statement shown later in this chapter. Therefore, it is very important to keep track of all your expenses before any discretionary spending takes place. For our purposes, we'll limit our discussion of discretionary spending items to four major categories (Internet, Television, Phones, & Dining Out).

Internet

While the Internet is listed as a discretionary spending item, it is rapidly becoming a need rather than a want as technology continues to transform how we work and play. The Internet now allows you the ability to take classes on-line, perform research, make purchases, do comparison shopping, share information, start a business, collaborate, and much more.

To obtain regular access to the Internet, you will likely have to pay a monthly fee. Like everything else, these expenses along with the features and benefits, can vary widely as noted in http://electronics.costhelper.com/internet-access.html. Based on this information, three basic options and their costs are listed below:

$10-$15 (Dialup)

$20-$45 (DSL)

$55-$145 (Fiber Optic)

For our budget example, we will choose the option that provides quality access at a reasonable cost.

Internet Access (DSL) = $30/month

Television

Technology continues to provide us with continual changes regarding new products and features, and television is no exception. The size and weight of TVs have undergone striking changes, while at the same time dramatically improving the viewing experience. This revolution has increased the demand for television programming that is good quality and variety. Subsequently, more consumers are willing to spend a good deal of money to access these services. Like other discretionary expenses, these can add a great deal to your monthly budget. The rate shown below is for a package on the bottom end of the scale regarding cable/satellite options.

$$\text{Cable/Satellite} = \$50/\text{month}$$

Phones

The telephone has probably undergone the greatest metamorphosis in both looks and usage. Phones were once confined to a stationary location and used by one or more people for talking. Now, they travel everywhere with us and perform a multitude of functions.

Like everything, there is a cost for the convenience and mobility that cell phones provide. This cost is made up of the price of the phone and the cost to access the cell phone provider's network. Phone companies realized early on that consumers may not be able to afford, or balk at, the costs associated with buying a phone. To get around this issue, the cell phone providers have the user pay for the phone over a period of time (usually two years) by charging a little more each month for the services. In exchange, the user appears to be getting a phone that is relatively cheap or even free.

Trying to determine the costs for cell phone usage for our budget purposes is difficult due to the variety of phones and services available. Therefore, our research focused on the monthly cost each month for reasonable service. The monthly cost of cell phone usage differed depending upon the survey with low of $47 to a high of $102. For our budget, we'll split the difference and use the following:

$$\text{Cell Phone} \quad \$\,75/\text{month}^*$$

* Assumes that cell phone has replaced the landline as the only form of phone service.

Depending on the services, these costs can quickly escalate into one your biggest discretionary expenses for the month.

Dining Out

According to the Bureau of Labor Statistics http://www.bls.gov/cex/csxann11.pdf the average consumer unit (2.5 persons) spent $2,620 in 2011 dining out. For our budget calculations, that works out to:

Dining Out = $87/month ($2,620/12/2.5)

To get a better idea of your food spending habits, keep your receipts for any food-related spending for at least a month. Use this information and enter it into the food spending calculator at:

http://www.motherjones.com/environment/2012/01/calculator-food-spending-budget-frugal

Per the website, "The result is this calculator, which allows you to see how your spending compares to that of others in the United States, your city, and various kinds of households and income brackets. You can also compare your budget to USDA recommendations."

The Bottom Line: Pulling it All Together

While each of the budget items discussed above is important in its own right, taken together they can help provide a complete picture of your finances. To see this more clearly, we have transferred each item discussed above into a (PIE) Personal Income and Expense Statement as shown in Figure 4.10. In order to see the effect taxes and expenses have on varying salary levels, we show someone making $20,000, $30,000, $40,000, along with an earnings amount to just break even. The resulting four budgets are derived from subtracting taxes and expenses from earned income as shown below.

```
+ Income          (Salary)
- Expenses        (Taxes and Expenses)
= Net Income      (Profit/Loss)
```

Figure 4.10 is divided into 3 main parts.

- **Green Area** - Shows Net Income[1] or the income left after payroll taxes are subtracted. This is obtained by subtracting Payroll Taxes (PT) from Gross Income or (GI-PT). Income and payroll taxes shown are annualized.

- **Yellow Area** - Shows Net Income[2] or the income left after payroll taxes and non-discretionary expenses are subtracted. This is obtained by subtracting Payroll Taxes (PT) and Total Non-Discretionary Expenses (TNDE) from Gross Income or (GI-PT-TNDE). As noted above, non-discretionary expenses are recurring expenses needed to live. For our purposes, these costs include housing, transportation, food, clothing, and personal care items. Also included in this category is health insurance. Due to forthcoming changes in federal regulations, it will soon become a mandatory expense that someone (employer or employee) must pay to be in compliance with current healthcare regulations. All non-discretionary expenses shown are monthly amounts.

- **Blue Area** - Shows Net Income[3] or income left after subtracting payroll taxes, non-discretionary expenses and discretionary expenses. This is obtained by subtracting Payroll Taxes (PT), Total Non-Discretionary Expenses (TNDE), and Total Discretionary Expenses (TDE) from Gross Income or (GI-PT-TNDE-TDE). All non-discretionary expenses shown are monthly amounts. The final net income figure (last line of Figure 4.10) shows whether any money is left over at the end of the month resulting in a green number, or if expenses were greater than income as shown by a red number.

Your Personal Finances

Figure 4.10 – Personal Income and Expense Statement

Income/Taxes/Expenses	Budget A	Budget B	Budget C	Budget D
Gross Income (GI)*	$20,000	$30,000	$40,000	$33,710
Payroll Taxes*				
Federal Taxes	2,554	4,054	6,375	4,609
State Taxes (3% Gross Income)	600	900	1,200	1,011
Local Taxes (1% Gross Income)	200	300	400	337
Social Security (6.2% Gross Income)	1,240	1,860	2,480	2,090
Medicare (1.45% Gross Income)	290	435	580	489
Total Payroll Taxes (TPT)	$4,884	$7,549	$11,035	$8,536
Net Income[1] Taxes (GI-TPT)*	$15,116	$22,451	$28,965	$25,174
Non-Discretionary Expenses**				
Housing				
Rent/Mortgage ***	560	560	560	560
Transportation				
Car Payment ($20,000 Loan)	377	377	377	377
Car Fuel Costs	203	203	203	203
Maintenance Costs	14	14	14	14
Automobile Insurance	72	72	72	72
Food budget/person	256	256	256	256
Health Insurance - Single Coverage	245	245	245	245
Clothing - Apparel/Services	86	86	86	86
Personal Care - Products & Services	32	32	32	32
Total Non-Discretionary Expenses (TNDE)	$1,845	$1,845	$1,845	$1,845
Net Income[2] (GI-TPT-TNDE)**	-$585	$26	$569	$253
Discretionary Expenses				
DSL Internet	30	30	30	30
Television - Cable/Satellite	50	50	50	50
Cell Phone – Service	75	75	75	75
Dining Out	128	128	128	128
Entertainment	86	86	86	86
Total Discretionary Expenses (TDE)	253	253	253	253
Net Income[3] (GI-TPT-TNDE-TDE))**	-$838	-$227	$316	$0

* Amounts shown are annualized.

** Amounts shown are monthly.

*** Amounts shown include expenses for utilities, operations, supplies, furnishings, equipment.

The taxes paid in each of the four different budgets (A, B, C, and D) in Figure 4.10 differ due to the variance in incomes. However, we kept the expenses the same for each budget for simplicity purposes.

Analyzing Your Options

If we look at the last line of 4.10, you'll note that **Budget C** (Income of $40,000) has a monthly surplus ($316) after all taxes and expenses have been deducted. This is the only scenario that generates positive cash flow (income is greater than expenses). **Budgets A** and **B** are unsustainable situations because of negative cash flows (expenses are greater than income). For these scenarios to continue, an accumulation of debt will occur, usually by means of a credit card.

To determine what each budget requires in terms of an earned hourly rate, we assume 50 weeks of work per year times 40 hours per week. This equals 2,000 hours worked per year and breaks down as follows:

- **Budget A** - $20,000/2,000 hours equals **$10 per hour**
- **Budget B** - $30,000/2,000 hours equals **$15 per hour**
- **Budget C** - $40,000/2,000 hours equals **$20 per hour**
- **Budget D** - $33,960/2,000 hours equals **$17 per hour**

To just break even (Income = Expenses) you would have to earn at least $17 per hour (**Budget D**). Unless you have some kind of post-secondary training (trade school or college) you probably won't be able to earn this type of money right out of high school. Assuming you don't want to go into debt, you have two options:

Option 1 - **Earn more money by:**

- Asking for a raise. Before taking this step, read our recommendations in Chapter 6 regarding how to prepare and properly position yourself for this type of negotiation.

- Working more hours.

- Working a 2nd job.

- Getting another job that pays more.

- Getting trained. This increases your value and relevance.

- Increasing your education. Does your employer pay for some or all of any tuition costs? If so, take advantage of this benefit. If not, is there room in your budget to cover this additional expense?

Option 2 - **Spend less money by:**

- Eliminating discretionary expenses where possible by asking yourself tough questions like:
  - Do I really need cable TV?
  - Do I need to eat out so often?
  - Can I get a cheaper cell phone plan?

- Cutting back on non-discretionary expenses where possible.

- Can you lower your rent by downsizing to smaller living quarters? How about sharing a house or apartment?

- Can you get by with a used car instead of a new one? Can you carpool or use public transportation?

You'll have to ask yourself these and other many other hard questions if you really want to eliminate unnecessary expenses from your budget. If we look at Figure 4.10 again, specifically **Budget B's** Net Income^2, you'll notice that someone making $30,000 or $15/hour almost breaks even (-$26) before any discretionary expenses are subtracted. Discretionary expenses are wants and not needs. Therefore, they should be reduced or eliminated where possible and can be the difference in whether your net income is either positive (**green**) or negative (**red**).

Our sample budgets in Figure 4.10 are just that, samples. When putting them together, we had to rely on a variety of sources and best guesses regarding taxes and expenses. While these numbers represent only averages, they're helpful in showing the basic elements of a budget and where improvements can be made. In order to make this relevant to your situation, you'll need to complete a budget that reflects your financial realities. That means:

➢ Looking at your paycheck, if you are working, to see what is being withheld in taxes.

➢ Determining the costs associated with your non-discretionary spending (housing, food, transportation, etc.).

➢ Determining the costs associated with your discretionary spending habits (dining, entertainment, etc.).

The information you obtain from your budget will only be as accurate as the information you put in to it. Therefore, it's important to take time to set up a system that will allow you to collect information as easily as possible. Our next section will take a closer look at the ways you can organize and track your finances.

Organizing and Tracking Your Finances

In order to remain fiscally sound, businesses use three financial tools to help them stay on track. They are the:

➢ **Income Statement** – Shows income and expenses over a period of time.
➢ **Cash Flow Statement** – Shows the inflow and outflow of money over a period of time.
➢ **Balance Sheet** – Shows the assets, liabilities (debts) and owner's equity of the company.

You'll have to do the same, if you want to ensure your future financial integrity. For our purposes, we'll concentrate on the first two because of their immediate relevance to your finances.

We already discussed the income statement as shown by our Personal Income and Expense Statement from Figure 4.10. You can make up your own using a spreadsheet program, download one from the Internet, or use an on-line version like https://pearbudget.com/spreadsheet.

The information that will go into your budget can be obtained from the sources listed below:

Checking Account

Similar to a cash flow statement that a business uses, your checking account shows the cash that comes into and flows out of your account. On-line banking has made this process easier by allowing you to view your account(s) in real time. While access to your checking account may be easier, it does not relieve you of the burden of accurately accounting for every transaction that occurs. Therefore, we recommend taking the time each month to balance your checkbook or on-line account. As noted above, this has historically been done by writing down all income and expenses via a checkbook. This process allows you to:

> **Did you know?**
> Bank customers may complain about hefty overdraft fees, but they're using the service more and paying the price. A new report shows overdraft revenue at banks, credit unions and thrift institutions totaled $32 billion last year. That's an increase of $400 million or 1.3% from 2011.
>
> Source: Moebs Services

- Get a better idea of your spending habits.
- Confirm the amounts being deposited and withdrawn.
- Provide better oversight and minimization of mistakes that can result in costly bank fees.

Transfer the information from your checking account into your budget. Entries shown just as a withdrawal can be tracked by saving the receipts from your cash purchases. This is discussed more in-depth in the following section (Receipts).

Receipts

While a checkbook is your check, or verification, against what the bank is displaying on-line and in bank statements, it doesn't provide a breakdown of all your expenses. Money taken out is just shown as a withdrawal and nothing more. Unless you keep track of all your purchases made with cash, you'll forget what that money was spent on. Therefore, get in the habit of getting a receipt for each cash purpose. Put them in an envelope. At the end of the month, organize into categories, and input them into your budget worksheet.

Credit Cards

Due to their ease of use and availability, credit cards are the preferred method for many to make purchases.

The good news on credit cards:

- The ability to track your spending. Purchases can be viewed on-line and are summarized in a monthly statement.
- They are often the only way to make on-line purchases.
- Can help build your credit history.
- They allow you to carry less cash.
- Can provide funds in case of an emergency or unexpected expenses.

The bad news on credit cards:

- Ease of use allows many to spend more than what their budget allows.
- Interest is charged on any unpaid balances at the end of the month.
- Missed payments can result in:

    - Penalties
    - Increased interest charges
    - A lower credit score

Therefore, we urge caution when using credit cards. If used, only charge what you can pay each month. Debt is easy to get into but very stubborn to get rid of. Thomas Jefferson knew the hazards of borrowing when he said, "Never spend your money before you have it."

Use the information (on-line and/or monthly statements) made available by your credit card company to help track your spending. Input these expenses into your budget spreadsheet along with the other information noted above.

Debit Cards

Think of debit cards as another way to pay by utilizing the funds in your checking account. With each purchase made by a debit card, funds are drawn directly from your checking account. If there is no money in the checking account, purchases cannot be made or an overdraft occurs, triggering additional bank fees. Used well, debit cards can curtail spending and increase tracking of purchases. Debit transactions will show up in your account and can be viewed on-line or in the monthly statements sent by your bank.

One expense that can slip through any budget is cash withdrawals made from a checking or savings account. Purchases made by cash can often go unaccounted due to a lack of documentation. When paying cash, get a receipt, place it in an envelope that is appropriately marked, and input this information into your budget. Or, record your cash transactions by using a simple three-column spreadsheet as noted below:

Figure 4.11 – Expense Tracking Worksheet		
Date of transaction	**Type of Purchase**	**Payment Amount**

This can be accomplished by using:

- Paper and pencil
- Electronically using a program like Excel
- On-line using Google Docs

You can create interactive forms that allow you to enter information into a spreadsheet using a form you set up in Google Docs. Adding new expenses is as easy as accessing an email link you set up. Instructions for setting up this process are at:

http://lifehacker.com/5939539/use-gmail-and-google-docs-to-track-anything

It does not matter what method you choose as long as you begin the process of tracking your expenditures. The information obtained from the above sources should provide a complete picture of your expenses. Your personal budget can be completed on a weekly, biweekly, or monthly basis. At a minimum, complete one each month in order to note the patterns in your spending habits. Concentrate on those expenses you can reduce or eliminate.

Paying it Down and Saving it Up

Based upon the results of your personal income and expense report, are you operating at a **profit** (income is greater than taxes and expenses) or at a **loss** (taxes and expenses are greater than income)?

Operating at a Profit?

Great news! Your cash flow is positive as more money is coming in than going out each month. This means you are running a profitable and sustainable enterprise. However, you should still see if any other expenses can be reduced or eliminated. More money allows you to pay down any debts (credit cards, car loans, etc.) or put toward savings.

Operating at a Loss?

Unfortunately your cash flow is negative with more money being spent than earned. This situation cannot be sustained for a long period of time due to the increasing accumulation of debt (meaning your reliance on credit cards and loans to get by). Expenses must be cut and the first place to look is your discretionary spending. Remember, these are wants, not needs and are therefore not necessary for your survival. If you can, reduce spending by looking at cheaper alternatives.

Ultimately, your goal should be to become debt free. Debt means you owe an obligation to someone else. Obligations must be paid back and that means you must earn money. That may mean less time and freedom to pursue your dreams and goals as you become enslaved to meet your monthly obligations. This can result in less time, energy, and motivation because you are running on the money treadmill. Dave Ramsey put it more succinctly when he said, "You must gain control over your money or the lack of it will forever control you."

One small change you can implement that may have a big impact on your finances is to use only cash or checks for purchases. This change will help you become more disciplined in your spending. It will also help you from adding additional amounts to your credit cards. This change in behavior must be followed by a plan to attack any debt you have accumulated. There are many ways to accomplish this and we list two of them below and what to do in the future:

- **The Interest Rate Method**

  - Make a list of all your debts and the interest charged for each.
  - Number them in order from the highest interest rate listed first to the lowest listed last.
  - Make the minimum monthly required payment for each debt.
  - Any surplus money goes to paying off the debt with the highest interest rate.
  - Once the debt with the highest interest rate is eliminated, move on to the next highest.
  - Repeat this process until all your debts have been paid off.

- **The Balance Method**

  - Make a list of all your debts and the account balances for each.
  - Number them in order from the highest account balance to the lowest.
  - Make the minimum monthly required payment for each debt.
  - Any surplus money goes to paying off the debt with the lowest account balance.
  - Once the debt with the lowest account balance has been paid off, move on to the next highest.
  - Repeat this process until all your debts have been paid off.

- **Saving for the Future**

  If you have been following our suggestions, you should be:

  - Tracking monthly expenses.
  - Constructing a budget from this information.
  - Refining spending habits to reduce expenses.
  - Paying down or eliminating debts.

Done consistently over time, this type of behavior will allow you to save for the day when you can't or don't want to work. It may seem like a long way off, but the sooner you start, the better your chances will be of having enough funds set aside for your retirement years.

One of the easiest ways to save is through your employer's 401(k) plan. Many employers will even match some or all of what you contribute, making your account grow faster. If your employer does not have a retirement plan, think about starting an IRA. It is never too early or too late to save for retirement.

This chapter is not meant to provide in-depth advice regarding what you should do with your money. The purpose is to help you organize, identify, and eliminate those expenses and behaviors that sabotage your financial health. Make it a priority to learn more about finances by visiting a website like http://www.kiplinger.com/. Many more can be found by going to http://www.nolo.com/legal-encyclopedia/content/best-personal-finance-websites.html. You must take control and learn what is best for you by reading articles that are applicable to your situation. Broadening your financial horizons will help to increase your freedom and security.

What's Missing?

Our PIE Statement is missing one expense that is increasingly becoming a larger part of many budgets, student loans. We chose not to include this expense because of the variable nature regarding amounts borrowed, if any. What we do know is that students graduating in 2012 with a bachelor's degree had an average student loan debt of $29,400. If this amount is paid off over 10 years, it translates into monthly payments of approximately $355. Adding this expense to the four budgets in our PIE statement in figure 4.9, would result in a negative net income for each scenario.

Use this information, as well as the information from Chapter 3 to make informed choices regarding any post-secondary educational training. If attending college is important to you, make sure it fits within your financial parameters.

Chapter 5 – Communication

"Half the world is composed of people who have something to say and can't, and the other half who have nothing to say and keep on saying it." - Robert Frost -

Great companies know the value of good communication. Internally, it's used to ensure the proper flow of information between all areas of the business. Externally, it's used to attract, inform, and persuade potential customers as you'll see in the next chapter. Candidates that can communicate properly and help the business achieve the objectives stated above are eagerly embraced. Unfortunately, many job applicants fall far short of employer expectations. This is reinforced by a recent survey of employers conducted by *The Chronicle of Higher Education* and American Public Media's *Marketplace*. It found applicants most lack skills in written and oral communication, adaptability and managing multiple priorities, and decision making and problem solving.

> **Did you know?**
>
> Communication skills are ranked FIRST among a job candidate's "must have" skills and qualities.
>
> Source: 2010 survey conducted by the National Association of Colleges and Employers

Because effective communication is so crucial to every aspect of your career, we devote an entire chapter to the various situations and circumstances you may encounter during your daily activities. Your ability to communicate will largely determine the amount of success you achieve, regardless of the endeavors you pursue in life. To efficiently cover every aspect of this topic, we have divided the chapter into two main sections: formal and informal communication. While each requires you to act and behave in different ways, they both play an important role in your professional and personal life.

Formal Communication

In its simplest form, communication involves one person sending a message (speaking, writing) to one or more people (listeners, readers). When both parties understand and comprehend each other, things get accomplished. Unfortunately, complexities can arise between sender and receiver creating barriers to effective communication. Often, employers intentionally place barriers in front of jobseekers in order to find the best candidates. These obstacles are tests designed to let the right people in, and more importantly keep the wrong people out. It's your job to overcome these barriers by communicating properly with many different people in a variety of situations each and every time.

We begin our formal communication journey by looking at one of the most important steps in your career, getting hired.

Pre-Employment

Prior to getting hired, your interaction with prospective employers will largely be limited to your:

- Resume
- Cover letter
- Application
- Interview (before, during, and after)

Because these items provide one of the few opportunities to make a distinct impression, it's imperative they contain the right information and be as accurate as possible. Therefore, we look closer at each, what it takes to get it right, and the methods you can use to distance yourself from the competition.

Resume

The first chapter of this book is devoted entirely to your resume and how you can construct the best one possible. Revisit this chapter to make sure your resume contains all the proper elements and information pertinent to the jobs you are applying for.

Cover Letter

> **Did you know?**
>
> The average attention span of a person in 2012 was 8 seconds.
>
> The average attention span of a goldfish is 9 seconds.
>
> Source: http://www.statisticbrain.com/attention-span-statistics/

Getting someone's attention is tough. Getting someone to look at your resume over several hundred other applicants is even tougher. Decreasing your odds even further are overworked managers with short attention spans, sifting through an ever increasing volume of applicants. Your cover letter is the key to overcoming these long odds by helping the reader connect the dots, in a short amount of time, before their attention is diverted elsewhere. Think of it as your long-distance sales pitch that will leave the reader wanting to hear more. Because it is so important, we recommend taking the time to learn how to write the best letter each and every time. If you haven't completed your resume, we recommend finishing it before writing cover letters.

The effort, work, and research needed to complete your resume will prepare you to write a cover letter that thoroughly describes your past accomplishments, reflects your best attributes, and connects your skills and abilities to the job. We look at the ways to accomplish that below.

The Basics

Before getting into the specifics of the cover letter, there are some basic operational standards you should follow:

Research

Find out as much as possible about every organization you are applying to by getting answers to questions like the following:

- What do they do?
- How do they do it?
- Are they hiring for other positions?
- Are they growing?
- How long have they been in business?
- What is the outlook for their industry?

- ➢ Who are their competitors?
- ➢ Has the current economy hindered or helped them?

Find the answer to these and many other questions. The information uncovered by your research will allow you to convey a more believable narrative as to why you are the best candidate.

Length

Keep it short and sweet like your resume and one page if possible. Can you write a persuasive letter that is to the point? Companies want candidates that can take large amounts of information, break it down, and communicate the important ideas in a succinct way. This is your first test and will show the employer just how serious a candidate you are.

Paper

Use the same paper used to print out your resume.

Fonts

Use the same type and letter size as your resume. Remember, the resume and cover letter are travelling companions. They need to look like they belong together.

Spelling/Grammar

This is one of those zero-tolerance issues. There is no margin for error. If these errors appear anywhere in your resume, cover letter, or application they will diminish, and most likely ruin, your chances for employment. Make it a non-issue by having as many people as possible carefully proofread your work.

Easy

Make it easy for the reader by spelling out exactly what job you are after. If you are unclear about what position you are applying for, don't expect the

Convey

While the resume is great for listing your accomplishments, it can be difficult to tell the reader everything about you in one page. The cover letter helps overcome this difficulty by giving you additional opportunities to highlight, clarify, and explain why you are the right candidate.

Enough

Leave some white space. Trying to jam too much into your cover letter, like your resume, will make it hard to read. Make it easy for the reader to do business with you or they will move on to the next candidate.

Attitude

Shows up regardless of how we communicate. Your cover letter has to ooze with enthusiasm. If you are not excited now, when will you ever be?

The Parts

As noted above, your cover letter is a sales pitch with the sole intent of landing you an interview. To get that interview and position yourself as a leading contender, three things must work in unison: the resume, cover letter, and job description. Because the job description is static, or unchanging, your resume and cover letter must align with, or highlight, key aspects of the advertised position. To show you how this all fits together we'll:

- Look at the five key points your cover letter must contain.
- Provide an example of each key point.
- Show you a finished cover that aligns with the resume and job description.

To do that, we'll use Figure 5.6 (Job Description of an Accounting Clerk) along with one of the sample resumes from Chapter 1 as shown in Figure 5.7. We'll use these items, and a step-by-step approach, to show you how to build a compelling cover letter.

Salutation

Write to a specific person where possible. If the job advertisement does not include a name, do some research or call the company to find out. If this information is unavailable, use "Dear hiring manager" or "To whom it may concern." The more you can personalize your letter, writing to a specific person, the better chance you have of getting noticed. For our example, we know the name of the hiring manager as shown in Figure 5.1 below.

Figure 5.1 (Salutation)

Dear Ms. Jane J. Candidate-Seeker,

Opening Sentence/First Paragraph

This is the chance to grab attention and hold it. If possible, use the name of a mutual friend or an acquaintance that helps link you to the job or company. Don't waste time starting your letter with the source of the job listing because that information should be in the Re: (Reference line of your letter). Remember, this is your chance to be different. State exactly what you want and how you would benefit the company.

Figure 5.2 (Opening Sentence/First Paragraph)

Michelle Goodsource, Career Services Instructor at CBA Community College, encouraged me to apply for this position. She noted that many of our past graduates currently work with you and have made important contributions to the company. I believe I can do the same as my qualifications closely align with the advertised Accounting Clerk position.

Notice how Jane J. Jobseeker used a person's name the hiring manager may or may not know but is associated with a school which has graduates working at the company. This information connects you with the company in some way and may help get you noticed. Not sure if you know someone at the company? Do a search on www.LinkedIn.com to find out. Use relationships, acquaintances, experiences, even recent news items to help you stand out.

Second Paragraph

Restate the key points of your resume and how your skills align with the advertised position.

Figure 5.3 (Second Paragraph)

My classroom knowledge was certainly put to the test during a six-week internship at ABC Accounting. Fortunately, my educational training allowed me to seamlessly move from solving problems in the classroom to providing real world solutions. Specifically, I was able to perform a variety of accounting and clerical functions such as statement reconciliations, ledger accounts, and accounts payable. I also worked on a team that reduced the average collection time on accounts receivable from 45 days to 31 days. As noted on my resume, I am at an advanced level with Word and Excel and plan to take the Excel certification test in the near future. My technical acumen, combined with a typing speed of 70 words per minute, allows me to perform accurate calculations at a rapid pace.

In this paragraph, we show how Jane J. Jobseeker's experiences and education, shown on her resume, directly correlate with items listed in the Job Description in Figure 5.6 and shown below:

- Reconciling statements to the general ledger
- Perform accounting and clerical functions
- Work with accounts receivable to collect past due payments

This paragraph also highlights three of the four items addressed in the Skills Preferred section:

- Associate Degree in Accounting or Business
- Advanced experience in Excel
- Ability to perform standard calculations rapidly and accurately

We have been able to directly link Jane J. Jobseeker's experiences and education with the job posting. The next paragraph will help continue to define Jane J. Jobseeker as unique and make her a front-runner for the position.

Third Paragraph

If your first two paragraphs didn't separate you from the competition, this one should. Talk about some of the details uncovered by your research. What did you find out about the company, industry, or relevant news? Use this information to highlight and discuss areas that are important to the employer.

Figure 5.4 (Third Paragraph)

Over the past several months, I have had the opportunity to speak with current and former employees of your company regarding employment opportunities. Encouraged by their comments, along with the recent rankings listing XYZ Resources as a Best Places to Work, I am excited at the possibilities of employment with your company. I am also encouraged by your commitment toward continuous employee training and would certainly welcome any chance to improve my skill sets as they relate to my future responsibilities with your company.

Our candidate, Jane J. Jobseeker, was able to convey to the hiring manager about her internal and external research on the company. This due diligence can help separate her from other candidates and make her a leading contender for the position.

Fourth paragraph

Summarize the benefits you bring to the employer and end your letter with a call to action. This is where you ask for an appointment. Being aggressive is a necessity. Sales are not made unless you ask the question. Therefore, ask for an interview or give them a time you will call.

Figure 5.5 (Fourth Paragraph)

> I believe my business and educational experiences make me a strong candidate for this position as well as a valued member of your team. I am eager to meet with you to discuss a plan of action. I will call your office next week to schedule a convenient time we can meet.

Our candidate's final pitch reinforces how her background relates to the advertised position and more importantly to the company, along with an assertive call to action. The complete cover letter is shown below in Figure 5.8.

Don't fall into the trap of using a cover letter template and modifying it slightly for each job. No two jobs are exactly alike and neither should your cover letters be. While it will take more time to write a unique cover letter for each job, it will help you more closely connect yourself to the job and increase your chances of success. Follow the recommendations above regarding what type of information should go in each paragraph.

Communication

> **Figure 5.6 – Sample Job Description**

Accounting Clerk

Location: Somewhereville, OH **Type**: Full Time
Department: Finance **Reports To**: Controller

Summary

Under the direction of the accounting supervisor, the Accounting Clerk performs routine accounting and clerical duties using established policies and procedures of the company. Operates standard office equipment such as typewriters, computers, facsimile machines, copiers, calculators, and any other machines required in the completion of duties.

Primary Responsibilities

Reconciling statements to the general ledger
Perform accounting and clerical functions to support supervisors
Research, track, and resolve various accounting problems
Record or post information in journals, files and/or other departmental records
Gather and sort checks and invoices
Enter invoices, checks, statements and other records into the computer
Work with accounts receivable to collect past due payments
Contact individuals regarding delinquent accounts
Provide assistance by answering questions and inquiries
Support accounting operations by filing documents, reconciling statements, using software programs

Skills Required

Possession of a high school diploma or its equivalent and preferably supplemented with some business school courses.

Experience with Word and Excel

Skills Preferred

Associate Degree in Accounting or Business
1-2 years of general accounting experience
Advanced experience in Excel
Ability to perform standard calculations rapidly and accurately

Additional Information

Must be able to pass a criminal background check.

We provide equal employment opportunities to all individuals without regard to race, color, religion, sex, national origin, age, disability, marital status, veteran stats, sexual orientation, citizenship, or any other characteristics protected by law.

Figure 5.7 Resume (College Graduate Without Paid Work Experience)

Jane J. Jobseeker
123 Main Street
Anywhereville, PA 12345
(123) 456-7890
jane.jobseeker@email.com

Objective

To obtain an entry level accounting position utilizing my education and internship experiences that will allow me to immediately contribute to the growth of the company.

Education

CBA Community College, Kroy, PA — wwww.cba.edu
Associate Degree/Computerized Accounting Management — May 2013
GPA 3.8/4.0

Relevant Courses:
- Principles of Accounting I, II, III, IV, V, VI
- Income Tax Preparation I, II
- Payroll Preparation
- Principles of Cost Accounting
- Accounting Information Systems I, II

Skills

- Typing Speed - 70 words per minute
- Mastery of MS Suite of Products (Word, Excel, PowerPoint, Access)
- Experience with accounting software packages (QuickBooks, Peachtree)
- Familiar with several operating systems (Windows, Linux, Mac)

Professional/Work Experience

Administrative Assistant (Six-Week Internship) — April 2013 - May 2013
ABC Accounting — www.abcaccounting.com
Anytown, PA 12345

- Entered, organized and reviewed data utilized in supervisor's reports
- Assisted in the preparation of financial statements and other related reports
- Performed a variety of administrative duties, including research, fact checking and organizing client files
- Assisted in the reconciliation of accounts receivable/payable and bank statements
- Worked with the finance team on yearly forecasting efforts

Honors and Activities

- Perfect Attendance Award - CBA Community College
- Accounting Award (GPA of 3.8 or higher) - CBA Community College
- Academic Honor Society - CBA Community College
- National Honor Society - Central York High School
- Honor Roll - Central York High School

Figure 5.8 – Sample Cover Letter

May 1, 2014

Ms. Jane J. Candidate-Seeker
XYZ Resources
123 Main Street
Somwhereville, OH 12345

Re: Accounting Clerk

Dear Ms. Jane J. Candidate-Seeker,

Michelle Goodsource, Career Services Instructor at CBA Community College, encouraged me to apply for this position. She noted that many of our past graduates currently work with you and have made important contributions to the company. I believe I can do the same as my qualifications closely align with the advertised Accounting Clerk position.

My classroom knowledge was certainly put to the test during a six-week internship at ABC Accounting. Fortunately, my educational training allowed me to seamlessly move from solving problems in the classroom to providing real world solutions. Specifically, I was able to perform a variety of accounting and clerical functions such as statement reconciliations, ledger accounts, and accounts payable. I also worked on a team that reduced the average collection time on accounts receivable from 45 days to 31 days. As noted on my resume, I am at an advanced level with Word and Excel and plan to take the Excel certification test in the near future. My technical acumen, combined with a typing speed of 70 words per minute, allows me to perform accurate calculations at a rapid pace.

Over the past several months, I have had the opportunity to speak with current and former employees of your company regarding employment opportunities. Encouraged by their comments, along with the recent rankings listing XYZ Resources as a Best Places to Work, I am excited at the possibilities of employment with your company. I am also encouraged by your commitment toward continuous employee training and would certainly welcome any chance to improve my skill sets as they relate to my future responsibilities with your company.

I believe my business and educational experiences make me a strong candidate for this position as well as a valued member of your team. I am eager to meet with you to discuss a plan of action. I will call your office next week to schedule a convenient time we can meet.

Best regards,

Jane J. Jobseeker

The Application

The application is discussed in-depth in Chapter 6 (Marketing and Selling). Specifically, you can find it in the section Managing the Process (Sales Pipeline) under Step 3.

The Interview

If you are diligent about completing your resume, researching companies, and writing effective cover letters, you will eventually be contacted by prospective employers. Although he lived more than 150 years ago, President Lincoln practiced these same organizational principles when he said, "I will prepare and someday my chance will come." When your chance comes, you must be able to effectively communicate your value to the employer, regardless of the interview format. Below, we look at the different stages of the interview process (before, during, and after) and how to be at your best irrespective of the format.

Before The Interview

If you are preparing for an interview, it means you have survived the first round of the tournament called the hiring process. In order to move to the next round, you'll need to be ready for your first real interaction (interview) with the employer. Because interviews now occur in many different formats (in-person, telephone or via video) you must be comfortable with each type. Before looking at the proper way to prepare for each, we look at the basic rules applicable to all interviews.

Pre-Interview Planning (Basics)

Practice – No one is a natural when it comes to interviewing. Functioning in this artificial environment is difficult in the best of times. To get better, you'll need to practice interviewing over the phone, using the computer (Skype) and face-to-face. Ask your guidance counselor, friends, or family members for help. If possible, have these mock interviews recorded so you can review the results. While it may be painful to watch, it quickly allows you to see and correct any mistakes.

Research – The best interviews are back and forth discussions that allow each participant to ask questions and express their viewpoint on a range of topics. This happens when both the interviewer and interviewee (you) are prepared. To be as prepared as the interviewer, we recommend focusing on the following three areas:

The company

Your job is to learn as much as possible about the company: their products and services, the industry they compete in, and the person(s) you are interviewing with. Prior research used to help write your cover letter should provide a good starting point. To be completely thorough, you'll want to look at:

- ➢ The company website(s) to find out where, what, and, how they make their products and services. Try and determine how long have they been in business as well as any other pertinent news.

- ➢ The Internet to find out who they compete against and whether their industry is growing or shrinking.

- ➢ Social networking sites like LinkedIn to find out as much as possible about the person(s) you'll be interviewing with. If possible, find out if you have similar interests, acquaintances, work history, etc. Making any type of personal connection with the interviewer can give you a decided advantage over your competition.

This type of research allows you to begin the process of integrating your experiences and skill sets with the needs of the company and will provide you with necessary talking points critical in an interview.

Questions you may be asked

Most interviewers will ask questions that seem very difficult, challenging, and designed to make you think on your feet. Why not be prepared for them? Examples can easily be found on the Internet by using search phrases like "tough interview questions." Look at the questions and see how the experts say they should be answered. How would you reply? Practice answering these types of questions until you feel comfortable and are able to provide thoughtful responses. The best types of answers appear genuine, are applicable to your situation, and reflect the logical steps in the decision-making process.

Forbes www.forbes.com recently listed ten tough interview questions and how they should be answered. Figure 5.9 shows three of the most frequently asked questions in an interview.

Figure 5.9 – Interview Questions That May Be Asked

Tell Me About Yourself

People tend to meander through their whole resumes and mention personal or irrelevant information in answering--a serious no-no. Keep your answer to a minute or two at most. Cover four topics: early years, education, work history, and recent career experience. Emphasize this last subject. Remember this is likely to be a warm-up question. Don't waste your best points on it. And keep it clean--?? No weekend activities should be mentioned.

Why Is There A Gap In Your Work History?

Employers understand that people lose their jobs and it's not always easy to find a new one fast. When answering this question, list activities you have been doing during any period of unemployment. Freelance projects, volunteer work or taking care of family members all let the interviewer know your time off was spent productively.

Why Should I Hire You?

The most overlooked question is also the one most candidates are unprepared to answer. This is often because job applicants don't do their homework on the position. Your job is to illustrate why you are the most qualified candidate. Review the job description and qualifications very closely to identify the skills and knowledge critical to the position, then identify experiences from your past that demonstrate those skills and knowledge.

Communication

The rest of the questions can be found at http://www.forbes.com/pictures/eglj45jhe/why-should-i-hire-you/

Questions you should ask

Asking questions accomplishes several things. First, it is a reflection of your level of interest in the job and the company. Second, it helps clarify the expectations of the role you will play within the organization. Finally, it allows you to differentiate yourself from the competition by using the special knowledge gained from your research to asked pointed and relevant questions. A good dialogue allows both parties to obtain a more accurate assessment of each other.

Alison Green, who writes the blog Ask a Manager www.askamanager.org, has a list of ten great questions that can be asked in an interview and are shown in Figure 5.10 below:

Figure 5.10 – Interview Questions You Should Ask

1. What are the biggest challenges the person in this position will face?

This question shows you don't have blinders on in the excitement about a new job; you recognize every job has difficult elements and you're being thoughtful about what it will take to succeed in the position.

2. Can you describe a typical day or week in the position?

This question shows you're thinking beyond the interview and visualizing what it will be like to do the work itself. This is different from many candidates, who appear to be focused solely on getting the job offer without thinking about what will come after that.

3. What would a successful first year in the position look like?

Asking this shows you're thinking in the same terms a manager does—about what the position needs to contribute to the team or company to be worthwhile. You'll also sound like someone who isn't seeking to simply do the bare minimum, but rather to truly achieve in the role.

4. How will the success of the person in this position be measured?

This question is similar to the previous one, but it will also give you more insight into what the manager really values. You may discover that while the job description emphasizes skill A or responsibility B, the manager actually cares most about skill C or responsibility D.

5. How long did the previous person in the role hold the position? What has turnover in the role generally been like?

If no one has stayed in the position very long, it might be a red flag about a difficult manager, unrealistic expectations, or some other land mine.

6. How would you describe the culture here? What type of people tend to really thrive, and what type don't do as well?

If the culture is very formal and structured and you're happiest in a more relaxed environment, or if it's an aggressive, competitive environment and you are more low-key and reserved, this job might not be a comfortable fit for you. You'll spend a large portion of your waking life at your job, so it's crucial to make sure you know what you're signing up for.

7. How would you describe your management style?

Your boss will have an enormous impact on your quality of life at work. While you can't always trust managers to accurately self-assess, you'll at least get some insight into their style by what things they choose to emphasize in response to this question.

8. Thinking back to the person who you've seen do this job best, what made their performance so outstanding?

Most managers' ears will perk up at this question, because it signals you care not just about being average or even good, but truly great. This is the question managers wish all their employees would ask.

9. Are there any reservations you have about my fit for the position that I could try to address?

This is a great way to give yourself the chance to tackle any doubts the interviewer might have about you, as well as for you to consider whether those doubts might be reasonable and point to a bad fit.

10. What is your time line for getting back to candidates about the next steps?

Always wrap up with this question, so that when you go home you know what to expect next. That way, you won't be sitting around wondering when you'll hear something.

Don't let the interview be a one-way conversation to nowhere. A few well-placed questions and comments will help set you apart from your competition.

Job Description – Reread the ad you originally applied to. How do the duties listed in the job description relate to your past experiences and accomplishments? This is a great way to begin formulating answers to possible questions that may be asked of you.

Resume - If you spent the proper amount of time getting your resume right, you should know it inside and out. Nevertheless, you should still have access to it during the interview for reference purposes. In Chapter 6, we show you a foolproof way to ensure you and the interviewer are looking at the same resume.

On-line profile – What does the Internet say about you? Find out by searching your name on Google, Bing, Yahoo, etc. What comes up? Does it accurately reflect who you are as a person? Do you think the results would impress prospective employers? Your on-line profile is largely determined by the information *you* put on the Internet and who *you* choose to associate with.

Many companies will do a quick background check by searching the candidate's name on the Internet. If they see something less than flattering, the chances of being disqualified are very high. How can you make your on-line profile help your cause instead of hurting it?

Discretion

One definition of discretion is "the ability to keep sensitive information secret." Are you using discretion when it comes to social media (Facebook, Twitter, Instagram, etc.)? Your input, pictures, content, and who you associate with contribute to your on-line public persona. While this information may seem irrelevant or funny to you, a prospective employer may have a completely different reaction. This information lasts for a very long time on the web. Don't let awkward images or negative comments sabotage your job search.

Control

Set up a LinkedIn www.LinkedIn.com account. LinkedIn is a professional networking platform that allows you to carefully craft a professional profile and connect with a variety of business professionals. Properly set up, it will often be the first thing an employer sees when searching your name.

Pre-Interview Planning (Phone)

> **Did you know?**
> Remote interviews and business meetings are becoming more common in today's workforce. According to a 2012 Census Bureau report, about 13.4 million U.S. workers currently work from home
> **Source: CNN Money reports**

Finding the right candidates, as quickly and efficiently as possible, is the goal of every employer. Phone interviews can shorten this timeline and help narrow the field to the most qualified candidates. Because this is a screening tool and determines whether you get to the next round, you must treat it with the same care as an in-person interview. Therefore, use the following tips to help you properly prepare:

Mindset - Act as if this is a face-to-face interview. Dress professionally if it will help your demeanor. Can you really sound professional in your pajamas?

Phone - If you are using a cell phone, does it get good reception in the area where you will be interviewing? Use a landline if possible and disable call waiting.

Speed – Slow down and speak clearly and evenly. This is even more important over the phone as the interviewer can't rely on body language to help determine what you really mean.

Quiet - Minimize disruptions as much as possible by having an area that will allow you to have an undisturbed conversation.

Pre–Interview Planning (Video)

As noted above, employers are using every method possible to shorten and streamline the interview process. Video conferencing, an approach that lies somewhere between a phone and in-person interview, is another tool employers are utilizing as a screening tool. It is also one of the most difficult interviews to get right. Because the etiquette is different for this type of format, you'll want to take the following into account to properly prepare:

Surroundings – To eliminate disruptions and distractions, pick a quiet location that is properly lighted and uncluttered. The latter is important because the interviewer will see what is directly behind you during the interview.

Programs – Close any open programs on your computer to minimize any disruptions.

Identification – Be aware of the message that your Skype user name and picture conveys. Unflattering and unprofessional names and images can leave a negative impression on the interviewer.

Clothes – Dress like you are going to an in-person interview. Although the interviewer won't see all of you, it is still important to project a professional appearance.

Connection – Use a wired connection where possible due to the less reliable nature of wireless.

Pre–Interview Planning (In-Person)

Contact Information – The company name, address along with the contact information of the person you will be interviewing with should be kept with you at all times. This is especially important in case you are delayed.

Format – Interviews generally follow two basic formats, structured and unstructured. In a structured interview, the same questions are asked to each candidate. This method allows an interviewer to easily compare answers from a large pool of candidate interviews. In an unstructured interview, the questions vary and are often used when the candidate pool is small. While you can't control the format of the interview, you can help control the dialogue by listening and responding in a way that aligns your abilities with the needs of the employer.

Questions - Great interviews provide an exchange of information that allows each party to make a more informed decision about a possible working relationship. Great interviewers make this happen by using behavioral and situational type questions that encourage dialogue.

Behavioral Questions

Your answers to behavioral questions reflect how you handled past situations and can be a good predictor of future behaviors. Figure 5.11 list ten behavioral type questions you may be asked. You can find many more examples of these types of questions by going to an article written by Dr. Tom Denham at http://blog.timesunion.com/careers/50-behavioral-based-interview-questions-you-might-be-asked/1538/.

Figure 5.11 – Examples of Behavioral Questions

1. Describe a time on any job in which you were faced with **stresses which tested your coping skills**. What did you do?
2. Tell me a time in which you had **to not finish a task** because of a lack of information. How did you handle it?
3. Give an example of a time in which you had **to make a decision quickly.**
4. Relate a time in which you had **to use your verbal communication skills** in order to get an important point across.
5. Describe a job experience in which you had **to speak up** to be sure other people knew what you thought or felt.
6. Can you tell me a time in which you felt you were able **to build motivation** in your co-workers or subordinates?
7. Give me an example of a specific occasion in which you had **to conform to a policy** with which you did not agree.
8. Describe a situation in which you felt it necessary **to be very attentive and vigilant** to your environment.

Communication

> 9. Provide an example of a time in which you had **to use your fact-finding skills** to gain information for solving a problem.
>
> 10. Give me a time in which you had **to set an important goal** in the past and tell me about your success in reaching it.

While it is good to know the types of behavioral questions you may be asked, you'll need a strategy to answer them if you want to sound convincing. Alison Green, from http://www.askamanager.org, says, "Here are four key steps to do before your next interview:

1. First, go through the job description line by line, and picture yourself doing the job. What will the person in the role be responsible for? What are the likely challenges?

2. For each responsibility or challenge, think about what examples from your past you can point to as "supporting evidence" that you'd excel at the job, and write them down.

    Keep in mind you don't need to be direct one-for-one matches. For instance, if you're applying for a sales job without any actual sales experience, you might talk about how you made fundraising calls to alumni when you were in college. Or if you're applying for a manager job and haven't formally managed anyone, you might talk about how you were the go-to person for training new employees in your last job, managed numerous group projects, and were known as a diplomatic problem-solver. And if you don't have a lot of work experience to draw on, you can use examples from school, volunteering, and hobbies.

3. Once you've written out your examples, turn them into answers that have this structure: problem/response/outcome. In other words, start by talking about why the situation was challenging. Then express what you did in response, and finally, explain what the outcome was.

4. Now, make yourself practice your answers out loud. You might feel foolish talking to yourself, but doing this will make these answers more easily retrievable when you're sitting in that interview chair.

Situational Questions

Situational questions are used to find out how you would act in a given situation. Figure 5.12 lists 5 examples of situational type questions and possible responses from www.quintcareers.com.

Figure 5.12 – Examples of Situational Questions

1. What would you do if the work of a subordinate or team member was not up to expectations?

Sample excellent response:

Luckily, I have quite a bit of previous team experience, and have faced this situation a few times in the past -- so let me tell you how I've learned to handle the issue. The most important first step in dealing with an underperforming subordinate or team member is honest communications -- talking with the person can lead to some surprising discoveries, such as the person not understanding the assigned tasks to being overwhelmed with the assignment. Once I discovered the problem, I could then forge a solution that usually solved the problem and allowed the work to move forward. So often in situations like this, the problem is some combination of miscommunication and unrealistic expectations.

2. A co-worker tells you in confidence she plans to call in sick while actually taking a week's vacation. What would you do and why?

Sample excellent response:

I would tell this co-worker that being dishonest to her boss, as well as her co-workers, is not wise, and being dishonest in her job is wrong. I would say how we all want more vacation time, but we have to earn it -- and that taking this extra time hurts everyone in the department because the person's absence will affect productivity. [contributed by Danielle S.]

3. Describe how you would handle the situation if you met resistance when introducing a new idea or policy to a team or work group.

Communication

> *Sample excellent response:*
>
> The best way to convince people is to be able to understand where they are coming from and address their questions and concerns about the new idea directly. It is also important to stay confident and believe in yourself because if you don't buy it, no one else will either. [contributed by Alexis]
>
> **4. What would you do if the priorities on a project you were working on changed suddenly?**
>
> *Sample excellent response:*
>
> I would notify everyone working on the project of the changes. I would then want to know why the priorities have changed, and if there is risk of them changing again in the future. I would then meet with everyone involved with a new strategy to address the new priorities. [contributed by Andra]
>
> **5. How would you handle it if you believed strongly in a recommendation you made in a meeting, but most of your co-workers shot it down?**
>
> *Sample excellent response:*
>
> I would continue to explain why the recommendation was good, giving concrete examples what the benefits of my recommendation could be. Ultimately if my co-workers continue to resist my recommendation I would have to let it go and move on. [contributed by Alexis]

More examples can be found at:

http://www.quintcareers.com/interview_question_database/situational_interview_questions.html.

Before answering these, and any other interview questions, it's okay to pause and reflect before speaking. Just be sincere and honest while answering.

Transportation - If you are driving to the interview, make sure your car is clean inside and out. Your car's appearance is a reflection of you. Why does this matter? There may be a chance, however small, that the interviewer could walk you to your car after the interview. If it is dirty or cluttered inside and out, it reflects poorly on you.

During The Interview

While the interview is one of the most sought after meetings, it is also fraught with fear and apprehension. Can the stakes get any higher, the competition any more fierce? One wrong word or thought uttered can doom your chances. The interview process, like anything else, can be mastered with preparation and practice. Below we discuss guidelines applicable to all interviews along with practical suggestions for each type of interview format.

Interview Guidelines (Basics)

Five Minutes - The first 5 minutes are crucial to your success. Tough questions may be lobbed at you immediately. You need to be ready to go right from the start.

Enthusiasm - Have some or you won't get the job. Employers want to see motivated candidates that are hungry and excited. If you aren't now, when will you ever be?

Style - You should be able to pick up on the interviewer's style pretty quickly. Adjust yours accordingly. For example, if they frequently use industry jargon, feel free to do the same.

> **Did you know?**
>
> The top ten most common mistakes made at an interview are:
>
> 10. Over-explaining why you lost your last job
> 9. Conveying that you are not over it
> 8. Lacking humor
> 7. Not showing enough interest or enthusiasm
> 6. Inadequate research about a potential employer
> 5. Concentrating too much on what you want
> 4. Trying to be all things to all people
> 3. "Winging" the interview
> 2. Failing to set yourself apart from the other candidates
> 1. Failing to ask for the job
>
> Source: www.careergeekblog.com

Responses – Be succinct but insightful when answering questions. If more information is needed, the interviewer will ask you to elaborate.

Notes – We suggest you jot down any key points you feel are relevant to the discussion. If possible, reiterate the important points during the interview and incorporate them in your follow-up letter.

Salary – Although this is normally not discussed in the first interview, it can be brought up by the interviewer at any time. Therefore, you must be ready to discuss or run the risk of undervaluing yourself during negotiations. Fortunately, this topic is covered more in-depth in Chapter 6. At a minimum, try and find the pay range of the job along with the prevailing wages of the area for similar jobs.

Interrupt - Unless your hair is on fire, wait patiently for a pause by the interviewer before responding or asking a question.

Pauses - Are fine when answering a question. Don't fill this time with ums and ahs. It's unprofessional and becomes obvious and annoying to the interviewer.

Closing - Don't let the interview end on a lull. Be prepared to have the last word and reiterate some key points on why you are the best candidate. Don Goodman of Careerealism www.careerealism.com suggests "it is also a good time to see if they have any concerns. Don't just end the call wondering how you did, ask them something like, 'Based on what we discussed today, do you think I am a good candidate for this position?'

Thank you - Always thank the interviewer for his or her time.

Next Steps – Ask about the timeline of the hiring process. This shows interest on your part and provides clues regarding follow-up.

Interview Guidelines (Phone)

Smile - Even though the interviewer cannot see you, smiling allows you to create a positive tone and tenor in your voice.

Interview Guidelines (Video)

Eyes - Look at the camera and not at the computer screen.

Notes – Feel free to use them along with your resume but know your stuff. You don't want to appear like you are reading from a prepared script.

Technical – Bring up any difficulties immediately if you are unable to see or hear your interviewer or if the connection is impaired in any way. You may need to terminate the session and reconnect. Have an alternate way to contact the interviewer in case you encounter any difficulties.

Position – The interviewer should have a good view of your head, shoulders, and hands. When starting the interview, take a quick look at the screen to make sure you are positioned correctly, and then concentrate on looking in the camera.

Smile – It can be harder to do when no one is in the room with you but is still a necessity to project a positive image.

Engaged – Just like an in-person interview, each person must be involved in the conversation to be effective. Be in the moment by periodically acknowledging your interviewer with appropriate responses. Don't allow the interviewer to become distracted by using long rambling monologues.

Interview Guidelines (In-Person)

Arrive - 10-15 minutes early

Cell phone - Turn it completely off

Padfolio - Bring something that will allow you to write on as well as store your resume.

Behavior - Don't joke, flirt, or play with your hair or face.

Consistency - Treat everyone you meet like they are the interviewer. A smile, firm handshake, and eye contact are a must for everyone. The interviewer will often ask other employees for their impressions regarding each candidate. This input helps the interviewer form a more complete picture of the applicant. Although you may have the technical skill sets to do the job, the employer also wants to know if you fit in and can get along with everyone.

Dialogue – We mentioned this several times before but it is worth repeating. Your goal is to turn the interview into a conversation so everyone involved can determine if you are the right person for the job. Having an honest conversation, where both parties have enough time to speak, allows that to happen. Look for talking points that correspond with your background, experience and education. Expand on them where possible and relate how your skill sets corresponds with the advertised position.

Practice - Although interviews aren't on the top of everyone's list of fun things to do, go on as many as possible. It will be time well spent. Eventually you'll start to feel more comfortable, be able to anticipate questions, and more easily tell your story. Once you reach this stage, you will start getting job offers.

Story - Be ready to tell yours. Pick out experiences that help highlight your value, make you unique, and relatable to the company and position. Stories interwoven with experiences are much easier to listen to than just a series of facts. Focus on being the problem solver.

Commonalities – Look at the job description again and note how it matches your education and/or background. It is your job to highlight these areas during the interview and why you are the best fit for the job.

Previous Employers – Saying negative things about your former employer(s), bosses, and co-workers during an interview is not advised. This type of behavior only works against you and will make you appear bitter and resentful. Time spent on the negative aspects of the past leaves you less time to talk about your accomplishments and future aspirations. Therefore, when you get a question like, "Why do you want to leave your current employer? Go positive with statements like:

> ➢ Growth opportunities are limited at my company and I want to pursue greater challenges.
>
> ➢ I am interested in working for a stable company that offers greater opportunities.
>
> ➢ The company is reorganizing and my department was downsized due to restructuring.
>
> ➢ Due to family circumstances, I have relocated to the area.

> My family obligations have changed allowing me to pursue full-time employment.
> I really wasn't looking for a new job but became aware of the opening, was intrigued, and wanted to find out more about what it entailed.

There are many ways to answer this question. Just be ready because it is one question you can count on being asked.

Ask – As noted above, the interview should be a conversation. That means asking questions. You should ask at least 3 great questions and not all at the end. If you are successful in turning the interview into a conversation, your chances of getting hired increase greatly. We listed several examples in Figure 5.10 above and many more can be found on the Internet.

Interview Guidelines (In-Person-Group Interview)

This type of interview is becoming more common and increasingly used as a screening tool when a large number of candidates are involved. The two types consist of candidate groups and panel groups.

Candidate group - This format has two or more applicants being interviewed at the same time. Because this process is used as a screening tool, you must try to differentiate yourself from the other candidates by:

> Trying to be the lead when answering questions.
> Giving unique personal details about you. Interviewers remember this type of information more often than stock answers received on the majority of their questions.
> Having prepared questions to ask.
> Interacting with your fellow interviewees if possible.
> Working as a team during problem-solving exercises but keeping your individualism where possible.

Panel Group – Under this format, two or more persons interview one candidate. This allows the employer to gain multiple perspectives and opinions from various interviewers. To thrive in this format, you should:

> Greet everyone individually, shake hands, and make eye contact.

Communication

- Don't focus on any one individual.
- Speak to everyone as you answer questions.

After The Interview

> **Did you know?**
> 58% of employers said it's important to send a thank you after an interview; 24% said it's very important.
> Source: www.careerbuilder.com

After interviewing, it's easy to feel like mission accomplished given all the work required in getting to this point (resume revisions, portfolio building, networking, company research, etc.). However, this is not the highpoint of your job search or the end of the sales process. Unless you were offered a position during the interview, your job is not finished. Proper etiquette demands you correspond with your interviewer(s).

Like most sales meetings, follow-up is essential if you want to close the deal. An interview is a sales meeting and you are selling yourself. Good sales people are relationship builders and know that every encounter helps strengthen that bond. You must do the same and follow-up with every interviewer. Failing to do so may remove you from further consideration. Industry statistics indicate that only 10% of job seekers follow-up after the interview. Take the following actions if you want to be different from other candidates:

Step 1 – Interviewer details. Make sure you have the following information before leaving:

- Interviewer's name and title
- Company address
- Phone Number
- Email Address

Step 2 – Ask about the hiring time frame. This will help you determine how and when you follow-up with the employer.

Step 3 - Send a thank you email the same day although not right away. Wait a few hours after the interview.

Step 4 - Send a letter via regular mail as soon as possible. This letter should:

- Reiterate your interest in the job
- Summarize your strong points and why you are a good match
- Clear up misconceptions, if any

Step 5 - Call 3-5 days after the initial interview

Step 6 – Contact the employer periodically for a status update but not so much that it appears like you are desperate.

If the interviewer specifically outlines next steps, use this to follow-up accordingly. At the same time, you should also:

- Alert your references and provide them with updates on your job search.

- Don't stop job hunting. Get as many prospects in the sales pipeline (discussed in Chapter 6) as possible. Having multiple job offers is a good thing and provides greater leverage in salary negotiations. The more leverage, the better your negotiating power.

- If additional information is needed from an interviewer, provide it as soon as possible.

Want to really stand out? Send samples from your portfolio after the interview. It is a great way to keep your name in the forefront.

During Employment

Up to this point, our focus has been on the value of communication during the job search process and the importance of representing yourself properly. While these skills (writing, speaking, and selling) are crucial in getting a job, they take on even greater importance as your career matures. Ultimately it is your ability to communicate effectively with co-workers, supervisors, and customers that will determine your success. In this section, we look at the variety of ways you'll communicate when performing your job duties. We start by looking at one of the most important parts of the process, listening.

Communication

Listening basics

To really listen, means being in the moment and fully attuned to your surroundings. It also means eliminating any distractions that occur:

- Externally - Put away cell phones, devices, and anything else that competes for your time. Dedicate this time and your complete attention to those who are speaking.

- Internally - Keep other thoughts from distracting you. Push them aside and refocus on the speaker.

To make it effective, you'll need to:

- Face the speaker
- Maintain eye contact
- Keep an open mind
- Respond accordingly

If you need more information, ask? Get clarification on anything that you are unsure of. The better the listener you are, the better your chances are of doing the right thing.

Regardless of the type of job you get, you'll be asked to communicate with many different people in a variety of situations. Each and every situation requires the use of proper etiquette intertwined with the company rules. Below we discuss the different ways you may interact with co-workers, management, and customers along with best practices for each.

Phone

The phone has, and will continue, to be one of the most effective ways to communicate internally with co-workers and externally with clients. Therefore, it is necessary to know how to use it effectively and efficiently. Because this method of communication is so critical to a company, you must learn how to use the phone system your employer uses. That means learning how to put someone on hold, transfer a call, and change your voicemail to name just a few. If instructions are not readily available, have someone teach you the basics until you feel comfortable.

Of equal importance is the company policy regarding proper procedures and phone etiquette. How are you supposed to answer the phone when a customer calls? Does it have to be answered the same way every time? If so, does the company have a script to be followed? Learn these functions as soon as possible to ease your transition into this new environment.

When Calling

- No gum chewing or eating.
- Identify yourself, the company name, and the reason for the call.
- Expect you will have to leave a message. This will help you organize your thoughts and allow you to leave a succinct message if necessary.
- If you have to leave a message, speak slowly and repeat your name and contact information twice.

When Answering

- Smile and identify yourself.
- Let the caller end the conversation since they initiated the call.
- Return calls as soon as possible. Does the company have a policy regarding when a call should be returned? At a minimum, a return call should be made in the same business day if possible.

Electronic

Email

Email allows information to easily flow internally to employees and externally to businesses in a highly efficient manner. In some cases, it has largely replaced regular mail due to increased delivery speed and lower costs. While the distribution method may have changed, the rules regarding proper communication must still be adhered to as noted below:

Sending

- Review - Read it at least twice before sending. Just like a letter, care must be exercised regarding spelling, grammar, and punctuation.

- Concise - Too many thoughts in one email can be confusing. Address only a few points at a time. You will get better responses.

- Recipients - If you have to send to more than one person and need a response from everyone, it is often best to send to each person individually. This personalizes the email and usually ensures a better response rate. If this is not possible, highlight the information you need, from whom it is needed, and by what date you need it. Be specific rather than ambiguous.

- Signature - Does your company have a specific one to use? A signature is personalized text (your contact information) that is automatically inserted at the bottom of every email message you send. If so, try and use when possible to save time.

- Recipient - Make sure the email is addressed, copied, and blind copied to the right person(s).

- Attachments - If they are really large, utilize another method for the receiver to obtain. Dropbox, FTP site, Google Docs, etc.

- Disclaimers - Like signatures, often appear at the bottom of all company correspondence. Does your company require them? If so, make sure you use the latest wording.

- Paragraphs - Just because we send this information electronically rather than by paper through the mail, it doesn't mean we get to ignore letter writing protocols. The same rules apply. Don't have one large mass of words with no breaks. Use paragraphs to separate thoughts. It needs to make sense.

- Humor - It's tough to be funny even when you are telling a joke in person. It is even tougher when trying to do it via email. Utilize discretion and save it for in-person communication. Be professional in all your correspondence and save the joke(s) for your personal time.

Responding

- Responding - Emails are like phone calls, they demand an answer. Reply to all questions and better yet, try to preempt further questions.
- Timing - Set aside specific times of the day to check and respond to emails. Responding immediately is probably not conducive to productivity and sets high expectations in the future. At a minimum, respond the same day if possible but no later than the next day.
- Questions - If you get asked the same questions frequently, save time by creating a template, point to links, or create a web page that addresses these questions.
- Chain letters - Are a form of personal communication. Do not forward them as it may make you look unprofessional and violate your employer's email policy.

Finally, emails are a great way to obtain and convey information quickly and conveniently. However, a back and forth sending of emails can occur without satisfactory resolution to the problem. Before this happens, pick up the phone or meet in person. Different problems often take a variety of approaches to get a resolution. Utilize the communication method(s) that will help you solve the problem in the most logical way possible.

Social Media

While often viewed as counterproductive, social media is becoming more commonly used as a way for employees to interact with each other. Rapid changes in technology now allow employees to exchange information with each other, their employers, and their customers. Because this type of media is relatively new, it's important to understand how it can affect your professional career. In this section we'll define it, look at the different types, and determine the proper etiquette for using social media in the work place.

Definition

The Merriam-Webster Dictionary http://www.merriam-webster.com defines social media as forms of electronic communication (as websites for social networking and microblogging) through which users create on-line communities to share information, ideas, personal messages, and other content (as videos).

The sharing of information occurs in three different ways through the use of:

Social Network Sites

Facebook – At last count, this social network platform had over a billion, and growing, active users worldwide. Initially started as way for individuals to share information with a network of friends, many companies now use it as well to interact with their customers.

LinkedIn – Discussed more in-depth in Chapter 6, this site allows users to construct a profile and connect with other business professionals. It can be a great way to keep in touch with former colleagues and build bridges toward future opportunities.

Media Sharing Sites

YouTube – This interactive site allows users to upload, share, and view videos. Because of its popularity it continues to grow at a rapid pace.

Flickr, Picasa, Pinterest, and many others – Are sites that allow users to share photos as well as other items of interest.

Thought-Sharing Sites

Blogs – Used by business to inform, persuade, and attract, they also can be set up by anyone as a forum for any topic of interest.

Microblogs – In contrast are made up of short sentences, videos, and pictures that are usually very informal, quickly created and consumed. Popular sites include Twitter, Vine, Instagram, Snapchat, etc.

Etiquette

Before writing anything to anyone — publicly or privately — ask yourself if you'd mind seeing it on the front page of the *New York Times*. That's exactly what Erin Grotts, director of internal communications at Supervalu tells her colleagues. "We tell people not to post anything that would embarrass you or the company...Would you be comfortable if it ran on the front page of the *New York Times*?"

Cynthia Beldner, Yammer community manager at Everest University Online, encourages her colleagues to ask, "Would I say this to my company's president and deputy general counsel in front of 1,000+ other employees?" Err on the side of caution on when and how you use social media.

If one or more of the above-mentioned types of social media are used by your employer as part of the daily business operations, follow the rules and procedures regarding its use.

Presentations

In-Person

Public speaking! Just the sound of these two words strikes fear into the hearts of many people. Flashbacks of standing in front of classmates while stammering through a report can be painful memories. All the preparation in the world could not get you ready for what seemed like a thousand pairs of eyes watching your every move. Sadly, this fear haunts many of us and hinders career growth and advancement.

Presentations, like most other aspects of life, are mastered with preparation and practice. Preparation is knowing the subject material, your audience, and relating the two in the most optimal way possible. Practice increases comfort levels and confidence allowing you to be as interesting and engaging as possible. The key is balance, utilizing equal parts preparation and practice.

The reason most of us are fearful of public speaking is due to a lack of balance. If you think about it, the majority of time spent in school is focused on learning new things. This is accomplished by listening to lectures, researching, doing reports and completing projects. Very little time is spent on telling others, outside your teacher, about your work. All your energy was focused on preparation and little, if any, went toward practice.

To rectify this imbalance and improve your presentation skills, consider the following:

- Know your audience - Being aware of this in the preparation phase allows you the ability to personalize the content and make it relevant to the audience.
- Make it a story - The best presentations use some type of narrative to engage the listener and make the information more relevant and meaningful to the audience.
- Keep it simple - Presentations heavily reliant on technical or industry jargon often leave even the most strident audience members in a daze. Make it in layman's (everyday) terms and invite those seeking more in-depth information to contact you privately. Winston Churchill knew this well when he said, "Know the big words, but use the small ones."
- Transitions - Using a visual aid like PowerPoint? Knowing your slides inside and out allows for easy transition from one slide to the next without looking. Visual aids should complement your presentation and not just repeat what you are saying.
- Rehearse - Again and again and again. Being properly prepared:

    - Will make you less nervous
    - More in command of the content
    - Allow you to better answer questions

- Want help? - Join a local Toastmasters group http://www.toastmasters.org. From their website: "A Toastmasters meeting is a learn-by-doing workshop in which participants hone their speaking and leadership skills in a no-pressure atmosphere."

On-line (Webinars)

Due to the increasing costs of physically gathering everyone in a room for a meeting or presentation, many companies are utilizing technology as the next best thing. While the format may differ, your presentation must still engage the audience and be as interesting as possible. Although this format may involve less anxiety than getting up in front of a room full of co-workers or strangers, it can be more difficult to generate the same level of interest and enthusiasm. Consider the following when presenting this way:

Before

- Preparation - give yourself plenty of time to properly prepare. While this will vary depending on the breadth and depth of the topic, plan on at least 10 - 20 hours of time in order to do a quality presentation.
- Time - What is the best date and time to give your presentation? Ask the participants by taking a poll.
- Software - Download any that is needed for your presentation. Practice using it to minimize technology glitches prior to the event.
- Instructions - Send to the attendees well ahead of the meeting and include with all periodic reminders.
- Practice - as often as necessary. Do a trial run to become familiar with your content, the software, and time needed for your presentation.
- Invitation - What is the best way to reach your audience? Email, social media, phone, etc. Use some or all of these methods to obtain the broadest reach possible. Make it easy to attend. Only ask the participants for their name and email.

During

- Time - Try and limit to 30 minutes or less. It is difficult to keep a room full of people interested for this long let alone staring at a computer screen.

- Key Point - Have one for every 15 minutes of presentation time. Given that the presentation should be about 30 minutes means no more than 2 key points per session. Need more time? Schedule another webinar.
- Images - If using presentation software, such as PowerPoint, don't just read what is on the slides The slides should complement rather than replicate your presentation.

Communication

- Engagement - Keep the audience involved. Try and ask at least one question every 10 minutes. For more effective feedback, don't just ask if anyone has questions. Be more specific and direct by asking something like, "How would this product help you work more efficiently?"
- Recorded Presentation - If so, let the participants know how to access after the presentation is concluded.

After

- Thank you notes - Send out right after the presentation.
- Reiterate - The main points of your presentation.
- Share - Any hyperlinks from the webinar.
- Feedback - Ask the attendees. Ask specific questions to get specific answers.

Meetings

While often maligned and considered inefficient by most employees, meetings remain a necessary function of business. Most often, they are used to inform, improve a situation, or solve a problem. Done correctly, they allow employees to provide input and play a role in the direction and success of the company. Unfortunately, many are poorly planned and fail to accomplish their intended goals. Because of this, meetings are often viewed as boring, unproductive, a waste of time, and help generate memorable quotes like, "A meeting is an event where the minutes are kept and hours are lost."

Did you know?

- 9 out of 10 people daydream in meetings.
- 60% of meeting attendees take notes to appear as if they are listening.
- 63% of the time, typical meetings in America do not have prepared agendas.
- It takes less than eight seconds for an idea, suggestion, or proposal to be criticized.
- Executives average 23 hours per week in meetings where 7.8 hours of the 23 are unnecessary and poorly run, which is 2.3 months per year wasted.
- 49% of participants considered unfocused meetings & projects as the biggest workplace time waster and the primary reason for unproductive workdays.

Source: http://www.yamlabs.com/blog/management_statistics_meetings/

There is a better way. With thoughtful planning and careful consideration, meetings can be a very efficient and productive way to get things done. To gain a better understanding of meeting dynamics, we will look at the roles you may play along with what should take place before, during, and after the meeting.

Meeting roles

Meeting participant - At first, you'll likely participate in many meetings before being asked to take the helm and lead the group. Use this time to observe the dynamics of a meeting and the role of each participant. The true value is having everyone participate in working toward stated goals. If you are a participant, it is your job to:

- Listen intently
- Take notes, if applicable
- Be prepared to provide input regarding any part of the agenda
- Participate in the discussions
- Complete any follow-up, if required

Meeting leader - It is your responsibility to run it in the most timely and effective manner possible. This requires careful planning and preparation before, during and after the meeting as noted below.

Meeting Procedures

Before the meeting

- Determine if it is really necessary. Does the benefit of getting everyone together outweigh the costs of taking employees away from their jobs?
- Distribute the agenda. This allows everyone to prepare and be ready to participate right from the start.
- Schedule during normal business hours if possible.

During the Meeting

- Hold individuals accountable for commitments from a prior meeting. Did they complete the work assigned to them? If not, why?
- State the **goal(s)** at the start of the meeting and agree to an **outcome** of each goal before the meeting ends. An example would be:
  - Goal – To create a new position in the sales department
  - Outcome – Determine the job description and salary range for the position

  This may be able to be accomplished during the meeting. If not, participants must be assigned specific tasks and the date it should be completed.
- Start on time and end before the scheduled time.
- Stay on task and on schedule.
- Avoid group pressure in the decision making process.
- Take notes or nominate someone to do it.
- Speak to express not to impress.
- Do not criticize a colleague in public.
- Schedule next meeting date, if needed.

After the Meeting

- Send the notes to all the participants and to anyone else affected by the actions of the meeting. Clearly indicate responsibility for any required actions.
- Follow-up individually with each person responsible for a particular action at the agreed upon time.

Teams

Like meetings, many view teamwork with a similar amount of skepticism because of poor past experiences. Often, much was expected and little produced due to a lack of direction and guidance regarding proper team behavior. Despite the bad reputation and pitfalls associated with teams, this working style is increasingly used by businesses to gain a competitive advantage.

Teams, like other aspects of a business, function more effectively when the ground rules are known by all participants. Whether you find yourself leading or just being a participant, below are some fundamentals of what makes an effective team:

Did you know?

- 39% of employees do not feel appreciated at work.
- 52% are unhappy about the amount of recognition they get.
- 69% of employees would work harder if they received better recognition.
- 78% said if they got better recognition they would be more motivated in their job.
- 49% said that if another company clearly recognized their employees, they would leave their current job.

Communication

> **Hierarchy** - Who is in charge? What role will each person play? These must be decided before any work can be accomplished.

> Source: http://www.thesocialworkplace.com/2011/08/social-knows-employee-engagement-statistics-august-2011-edition/

> **Goal(s)** - What are they, what time frame, and when will the team know when they are finished?

> **Communication** – Will largely determine the success of the team. Because each member is there for a reason, they need to communicate effectively with all their fellow team members. Will it be via face-to-face meetings, email, forums, webinars, or a combination of these? How often will you need to communicate: daily, weekly, monthly? Ask the other members, gain a consensus, move forward, and adjust if necessary.

Be aware that teams can take a great deal of time and energy to set up and maintain. However, they are well worth it as successful teams far outperform the efforts of a group of people just working individually. To increase your chances of success, carefully choose individuals committed to being honest, flexible, reliable, and willing to share.

Recognition

Isn't it rewarding to be recognized for an achievement? We all want to feel needed, respected and appreciated for the contributions we make. Mother Theresa recognized this when she said, "Kind words can be short and easy to speak, but their echoes are truly endless." Too often though, we feel unappreciated, undervalued, and even ignored as many companies fail to understand the connection between recognition and employee motivation. Conversely, great companies know that employees are their most valuable resource and consistently acknowledge their contributions.

When starting your career, you will likely have little input on how your employer recognizes its employees for their achievements. However, this should not discourage you from identifying the efforts of your fellow employees. Below we look at the different ways in which you can acknowledge your fellow co-workers.

Specifically, we look how you, in the role of employee or manager, can have a tremendous impact on the people you work with.

You - As the Employee

As an employee, your main focus has to be on performing your job (*hard skills*) to the best of your ability and to the satisfaction of your manager. However, to grow both professionally and personally demands that you also be adept at human relations (*soft skills*). That is the ability to communicate, collaborate, and negotiate properly depending upon the situation. In order to do this on a consistent basis and in a professional manner, you'll need to incorporate the following into your daily routine:

- Manners - Never go out of fashion and should not be used sparingly. Using please, thank you, and appropriate daily greetings (good morning, good night, etc.) not only reflect proper etiquette but show respect for your co-workers.

- Credit - Should be given where it is due. Don't use the ideas of others without giving them full credit. This type of behavior only leads to distrust and discord with your fellow employees. Harry Truman, the 33rd president of the United States, realized the value of working with selfless people when he said, "It is amazing what you can accomplish if you do not care who gets the credit."

- Write - Periodic notes to your co-workers thanking them for their help and support. Email is good but a handwritten note is even better.

- Know - The people you work with. Periodically inquire about their life outside of work. This shows you value them not only as a colleague but as a person. However, use discretion as no two people are similar. Some will be more open about their personal life than others.

You - As the Manager

A good manager knows they will ultimately be judged based upon the efforts of his/her employees. Orrin Woodward said it more eloquently when he stated, "A leader is always first in line during times of criticism and last in line during times of recognition."

Recognizing employees has many positive effects with the most powerful being motivation. One of the easiest and most cost effective ways to accomplish this is by having a recognition program in place. Done correctly, it places value on employees' hard work and provides direction and emphasis on attainable company goals. While it can range from a simple thank you to formal recognition programs, the important point is to have something in place.

What makes up a good recognition program? What do employees value? A great place to start is by asking. Asking employees for input generates new ideas and helps promote buy-in. Regardless of what is implemented, consider the following in making it effective and as easy as possible to administer:

- Make sure the rules are published and known by everyone.
- Make sure the award is in proportion to the level of achievement.
- Don't be vague regarding expectations and awards.
- Have a process to follow to avoid any sense of unfairness.
- Include everyone. Make the recognition culture as wide as possible by not overlooking any employee or classification level.
- Have a budget and revise when necessary.

One of the easiest, cheapest and most effective ways to recognize individual contributions is by simply writing a note. As noted previously, emailing your appreciation is acceptable but hand written notes tend to convey more gratitude. To be effective using this approach, thank the person by name and the reason for the recognition. If applicable, state how their behavior:

- Made you feel.
- Helped the team or organization.
- Helped the organization reach its goals.
- Finally, thank the person again in closing.

There is no hard and fast rule in recognizing employees because each person responds differently. Getting to know your employees will help determine the most appropriate ways to recognize their behaviors. Any effort you make will go a long way in generating the good will of your employees.

Post-Employment

Begin with the end in mind! Anyone thinking about starting a business is encouraged to do just that. While the vast majority of a business plan is dedicated toward starting and running a profitable business, a portion of the plan has to address the exit strategy of the owner. An exit strategy is a plan outlining what will happen when the owner leaves the company. Some of the more common options are to sell, close, or transfer the business.

Do you have an exit strategy? Based upon a very revealing fact compiled by the Bureau of Labor Statistics, you'll need to. They found in 2010, the average person had been with their current employer only 4.4 years. If the average working span of an individual lasts approximately 40 years, you may end up working for possibly 9 or 10 different employers.

Because you may be employed at many places over the span of your career, it's important to have a plan of action in place for several reasons. First, it shows your level of professionalism and the value you place on past, present, and future relationships. Second, it allows you to rely on past employers to verify your work history and provide letters of reference and recommendations. Third, it provides continuity and context throughout your career and further establishes the integrity of your brand. Finally, it may provide you with the opportunity of returning to your former employer if needed.

Before leaving any job, we recommend that you take the time to *evaluate* your current situation, determine if any *changes* are possible, follow the correct *rules of departure*, and act accordingly throughout the entire process (*do's and don'ts*). These are discussed in greater detail below:

Evaluate

Based upon the information from the Bureau of Labor Statistics noted above, it's highly likely you will work for many different employers during your career. The good news, this trend means you're less likely to remain trapped in a job that is not right for you. The bad news, it may be too easy to be a job jumper instead of truly evaluating your circumstances. Before making a change, it's worth taking the time to evaluate your current situation. Is quitting the right answer? Carefully consider the following before making a change:

- **Employees** – Are the people you work with generally happy, and feel respected?
- **Management** – Do they ask for and value employee ideas? Are they fair and consistent with everyone? Do they believe in the mission of the organization and try to live by its rules?
- **Training** – Is it offered on a consistent basis or when needed? Are industry standards followed at all times?
- **Accomplishments** – Are employees regularly recognized and appreciated for their contributions?
- **Communication** – Does information easily flow from management to the employees and vice versa. Does management have an open door policy?
- **Turnover** – Is it low, high, not an issue?
- **Compensation** – Is your pay in line with what other companies pay for your position? Do you regularly get performance reviews and corresponding increases in salary?

Changes

You owe it to yourself to make an honest evaluation of your current employment situation to see if any changes can be made. Answering the questions posed in the previous section will help you do that. If it is a new job, give it some time. At a minimum, several weeks should be spent observing and asking questions. What looked like chaos in the first few days on the job may make more sense and even seem logical the longer you are there. After you have been there a while:

- Make reasonable changes within the scope of your work that are beneficial to your processes. Most jobs have some range of autonomy (independence or freedom) an employee can exert in the performance of duties.
- Work with co-workers to improve systems and procedures. Be aware that resistance to change is universal, so start slow. Take the initiative, in a

nonthreatening way, and show how improvements in processes can save time, energy, and make the company more profitable. While this process can be very slow, it provides invaluable experience to your career. You'll learn a whole lot more when working conditions are not ideal than you will when stepping into a highly efficient operation.

- Work with your supervisor or hiring manager. They hired you for a reason and want you to be as productive as possible. They should know the description of the job you are to do, and should help you in any way possible to get that job accomplished. Your job is to work as efficiently and effectively as possible. If you can make improvements, let your manager know. Worst case, they reject your ideas and say no.

If you have made a reasonable effort to change your area of responsibility and continually get resistance from your co-workers, supervisor and management, you may need to start planning your exit strategy. Below we list the rules to follow when contemplating a job change.

Rules of Departure

- **New Job** - The first and most important rule, always have another job before you quit your present one. Having a job, while looking for another, allows you to be more selective and provides great leverage when negotiating salary and benefits with the new employer.

- **Letter** - Upon acceptance of a new job, compose a resignation letter. It doesn't have to be long or wordy but should cover 3 main points.

    1. When you are leaving
    2. Why you are leaving
    3. Conclude with words of appreciation

This letter does several things. First, it allows you to formulate your thoughts into cohesive talking points. Second, it provides the employer with formal documentation and the specifics of your pending departure. Third, it can allow you to express your feelings more easily in writing than by having to verbalize them.

- **Face-to-Face** - Your immediate supervisor or manager needs to be the first to hear the news because it directly affects his or her job. He or she deserves to hear it from you in-person and not via email, phone, or the various forms of social media. Unless it is extraordinary circumstances, anything but a face-to-face discussion is bad etiquette and taints your legacy.

- **Advance notice** - Give at least the standard two-week notice but be aware a longer notice may be required and depends upon your position. Before accepting a new job, think about the time needed by your current employer to adequately replace you. If it will require more than two weeks, mention this possibility to your new employer during negotiations.

- **Wrapping Things Up** - How much notice should you give your present employer? This will often depend on your negotiations with your future employer. Will you be teaching someone else about your duties? If so, how much time will it take? Do you need to wrap up a current project? How about the transfer of your knowledge to someone else? Answering these types of questions will allow adequate preparation by both your past and future employers. The more seamless the transition, the better your legacy will be.

- **Property** - Collect all your personal property prior to your last day of employment. If you think you will be shown the door immediately upon resigning, begin slowly taking a few things home with you each night.

- **Attitude** - Don't be negative or gloat about leaving. Even if your time with the employer was less than agreeable, be as pleasant and helpful as possible. Take the high road and go out on a winning note.

Do's and Don'ts

We close this section by looking at what to do (Do's) and not to do (Don'ts) when leaving a job.

Do:

- Honor all of your commitments and obligations to your current employer
- Leave with dignity
- Offer assistance with any transitions

- Ask for references or letters of recommendation if appropriate
- Allow the employer to address any of your concerns before leaving
- Participate honestly in any exit interviews
- Get answers to any of your questions before leaving (last paycheck, Cobra, payment for unused vacation, sick time, etc.)

Don't

- Post that you got a new job on any social media websites until you tell your current employer first.
- Take any sick or vacation days after you have given notice.
- Look for a new job on company time.
- Share proprietary information from your old job with your new employer.
- Conspire with others to leave with you.
- Incapacitate the company in any way by deleting data, breaking machines, etc.

Informal Communication

Great minds discuss *ideas*, average minds discuss *events*, and small minds discuss *people*. - Eleanor Roosevelt -

Strip away all the rules, hierarchies and organizational charts. Remove the formal policies, procedures, and routines. What's left? Informal communication that is free flowing, non-scripted, and occurs anywhere and everywhere. Its value lies in filling voids left uncovered by an organization's formal communication policies and takes place naturally when people work together in close proximity. In the past, it was done solely through talking in person or over the phone. Changes in technology now allow it to happen in a multitude of ways through texts, tweets, emails, chat rooms, instant messages, forums, and so on.

While we have discussed at length the importance of communicating formally in getting, keeping, and leaving a job, we also need to realize the importance of informal communication in the workplace. In this section, we'll look at the positives and negatives regarding informal communication, the proper rules regarding its use, and finally how to be a better communicator.

Positives of Informal Communication

For many, daily communications at work are relaxed, informal, and spontaneous. It yields many positives that in turn:

- Allow us to learn from our co-workers.
- Provide a medium for collaboration.
- Help satisfy social and emotional needs.
- Reduce time with spontaneous and rich interactions.
- Help clear up any misunderstandings regarding company communication.

Negatives of Informal Communication

However, left unchecked or used incorrectly, informal communication can:

- Undermine the use of proper procedures.
- Foster an "us" vs. "we" attitude.
- Easily spread and amplify false information.
- Provide a vehicle where unhealthy gossip thrives.

Rules of Informal Communication

Many careers have been sidetracked, damaged or even ruined for failing to distinguish the differing roles communication plays in a company. Mark Twain knew this all too well when he said, "Better to remain silent and be thought a fool than to speak out and remove all doubt." Given that words can remain forever due to the various technologic innovations noted above, we suggest you err on the side of caution. Use the following rules of engagement regardless of the situation or medium in which you choose to express your thoughts.

> **Did you know?**
>
> About two-thirds of our conversation is devoted to social topics—talking about ourselves and others.
>
> Statistics show individuals spend an average of 65 hours per year gossiping and 61% of the workforce engages in this activity.
>
> **Source: Robin Dunbar, Professor of Evolutionary Anthropology at the University of Oxford**

- **Audience** - Who are they? Co-workers, employees, or supervisor? Treat each with respect and adjust your language accordingly.
- **Assume** - anything you say will be repeated to anybody or everybody.
- **Confidence** - is earned not given. Know who you can trust before disclosing personal or private information.
- **Authentic** - Don't be fake or phony. People can spot a disingenuous person a mile away. Take a sincere interest in the people you work with.
- **Whining/Blaming** - Avoid at all costs. There is no upside to these types of behavior and will hurt your career. Show leadership by:
    - Being grateful instead of complaining.
    - Taking personal responsibility for your actions.
    - Finding solutions to problems.
- **Over Communicate** - Don't spend so much time talking it hurts your productivity and the others around you. Be respectful of others instead of monopolizing the conversation.
- **Boundaries** - It is a fine line to inquire about your co-workers' personal lives and knowing too much. Be judicious by showing you care but not so much you appear meddlesome.

Be a Better Communicator

Good communication skills never go out of style and are often the deciding factor in many hiring decisions. Employers continually search for candidates who can speak, write, and interact with a wide range of people in many different ways. To get better at communicating:

> - **Read** – as much as possible. Set aside time each day to stay informed and learn about new things.

> - **Write** – daily and be cognizant of proper grammar and spelling. To be a good speaker, you must put in time as a reader and writer.

> - **Listen** – to those around you and learn from the ones who can communicate properly.

To get better, practice, take a class, and gravitate toward those who exhibit good communication skills. If you want to be successful, surround yourself with successful people. Jim Rohn said it more eloquently when he famously declared, "You are the average of the five people you spend the most time with." Surround yourself with those people that practice the habits mentioned above.

Chapter 6 - Marketing & Selling Yourself

"Doing business without advertising is like winking at a girl in the dark. You know what you are doing but nobody else does." - Steuart Henderson Britt -

The first five chapters have set the table for our final topic, marketing & selling. Up to this point, our gaze has been inward with the goal of getting you (the product) in the best shape possible to get the best job possible. To accomplish this, we have concentrated on five specific areas covered in the preceding chapters. They have required you to:

- Summarize your credentials into a fascinating **resume**.
- Assemble artifacts into a **portfolio** that highlights your accomplishments.
- Learn more about yourself, your passions, and the role **education** plays in helping you reach your professional and personal goals.
- Realize the importance of **personal finances** and the consequences it can have on all aspects of your life.
- Learn the correct way to **communicate** each and every time regardless of the situation.

In other words, the focus has been on organizing your skills and abilities into a cohesive format that is attractive to potential employers. We now shift our view outward and look at the best ways to present you (the product) to the market place. We'll do this by comparing the sales and marketing activities of a business and how they relate to your job search efforts.

It's not enough to just list your skills and qualifications on your resume, post it to one of the large job boards (CareerBuilder, Monster, etc.), and wait for someone to call. That can turn into a very long wait with little or nothing to show from it. To find, apply, and be considered for the best jobs requires a great deal of effort. Your effectiveness, in getting job offers, will largely be determined by how well you manage the following activities.

- Marketing - Generating Interest
- Managing - The Job Search Process
- Selling - Closing the Deal

Because these three areas are vital to your success, we take a greater look at each in this chapter.

Marketing - Generating Interest

Marketing, as defined by Wikipedia, "is the process of communicating the value of a product or service to customers." Look around and you'll see it everywhere you turn (TV, the Internet, radio, billboards, clothing, signs, buses, cars, you name it). You are literally bombarded with hundreds of messages, maybe even thousands, from the time you get up in the morning until you go to bed at night. Why so many ads all day, every day? Businesses want your attention. They want it so badly $140 billion was spent in the USA on advertising in 2012 according to kantarmediana.com. Once a business *attracts* your attention, they can then *inform* you of their product, and hopefully *persuade* you to buy. *Attract, Inform, Persuade.*

While companies have the luxury of relying on a variety of marketing methods to gain the attention of prospective customers, you really only have to focus on one. Your resume! It is still the most accepted, and often the only, way to inform prospective employers about what you have to offer. It must, like any other form of advertising, do three things for you. *Attract* the attention of employers, provide *inform*ation to them about yourself, and *persuade* them to contact you for an interview. *Attract, Inform, Persuade.*

The good news, technology has made it easier than ever to get your message into the hands of many companies in a short amount of time. The bad news, most companies are inundated with resumes making it very difficult to get noticed. How can you stand out from the crowd? Later in this chapter, we cover the techniques and methods to effectively market you in today's business climate. However, before we do that, we have to make sure that you (the product) will be acceptable to the marketplace (employers).

Some companies make the mistake of spending a great deal of time and money marketing a product before knowing whether the customer will actually like it. If it doesn't sell, it is the customers' way of saying the product or service does not provide enough value. The reverse is true if the business successfully sells its product. In other words, it punishes those with poor products and rewards those with better ideas. Therefore, you must make sure your product offering brings value to prospective employers. In order to do that, we'll follow the marketing template used by many businesses.

The Four P's of Marketing

The Four P's, also known as the marketing mix, are four elements of a strategy used to promote a particular product or service. Up to this point, we have only discussed marketing in very general terms. Now we dig a bit deeper to see what is required in making a viable product that will sell in the marketplace. The process is started by trying to answer the following four questions:

1. What am I selling? **(product)**
2. How much is it? **(price)**
3. Where am I selling it? **(place)**
4. How will the customer find out about me? **(promotion)**

Answering these questions help lay the groundwork for what will be the overall strategy or marketing mix for a product. Done correctly, it helps a company stand out from its competitors. In effect, it begins the process known as "Branding" and defined by Wikipedia as "the name, term, design, symbol, or any other feature that identifies one seller's good or service as distinct from those of other sellers." In the past, this term has been associated with a product, service, or company. Increasingly, it is a term applicable to an individual, is built (consciously or unconsciously) throughout a career, and is based on the actions, words, and associations of that person.

A brand, like a reputation, can take years to build and seconds to lose. Therefore, it requires you to be deliberate in your actions, discreet with your words, and very thoughtful in regards to your professional relationships. To begin building your brand, you must be able to answer questions like:

- What makes me unique?
- How am I different?
- What are my best qualities?
- Why should someone want to hire me?
- How do I bring value to an organization?

Is it your education, experience, or integrity that makes you different? Thinking about the answers to these and other similar questions will help you begin to identify your differentiators. These are the things that make you unique and stand out from the crowd. Knowing the answers to these types of questions will help you respond quickly, sincerely, and confidently during interviews. The work required in writing your resume and building a portfolio will help with this process.

We now look at the four parts of brand building (product, price, place, and promotion) to see how you can be as compelling as possible to prospective employers.

Product

As noted earlier, appearance matters. Not only must you deliver as promised, but be packaged correctly as well. To help present yourself in the best possible way, we focus on the following:

- **Appearance** (product packaging) - How to properly present yourself in an interview.
- **Diet** (product ingredients) - How health can affect your ability to get and keep a job.
- **Fitness** (product durability) - How to perform at optimum efficiency throughout your career.

Appearance (Product Packaging)

Pick me up and look me over, better yet, buy me. That's the ultimate goal of every business selling a tangible product. Effective packaging can be the difference in whether a product turns a profit or loses money. Therefore, a great deal of time, money, and research goes into the packaging of a product. While companies accentuate the uniqueness of their products to get noticed, you'll need to strive for a conventional appearance. Your appearance should conform to current standards of interview attire and thus complement your actions and words.

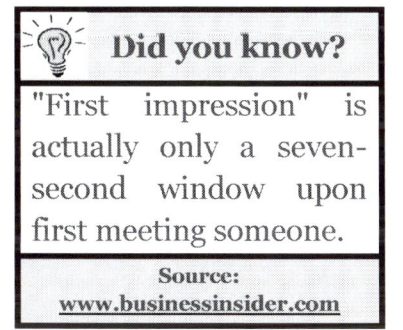

> **Did you know?**
> "First impression" is actually only a seven-second window upon first meeting someone.
> Source: www.businessinsider.com

Because all the attention is focused on you during an interview, every aspect of your appearance will be scrutinized. If properly attired, attention will quickly be drawn toward what you have to say and not what you look like. Your appearance may only play a supporting role, but it is still crucial in conveying your professionalism and commitment. Make sure it doesn't disqualify you before getting a chance to make your case as to why you are the best candidate.

While the first few seconds upon meeting someone are critically important, John Lees of http://www.johnleescareers.com/ says, "The idea that employers decide to hire or reject in the first 30 seconds of an interview is an urban myth. If it were true, interviews would be much shorter. What happens is that an interviewer makes initial decisions about your personality which are fairly hard to shake." Your job is to make the interviewer's job as easy as possible by having a flawless appearance. In order to help you accomplish this, we have divided appearance into three sections (proper interview attire, what not to bring, and interview tips).

Proper Interview Attire (Women)

- Clothes - Navy, black or dark grey suit
- Shirt - Coordinated matching blouse
- Shoes - Conservative and coordinated to match clothes
- Jewelry - Little or none. Preferably only earrings
- Hairstyle - Professional
- Pantyhose - Neutral
- Makeup - Light
- Perfume - Light. Used sparingly or not at all.
- Nails - Manicured
- Portfolio/briefcase

Proper Interview Attire *(Men)*

- Clothes - Solid color suit (navy or dark grey)
- Shirt - White or light blue
- Belt - Black or brown to match your shoes
- Tie - Conservative. Good quality silk
- Socks - Dark, mid-calf length
- Shoes - Conservative style in black or brown that is either slip-on or lace-up.
- Jewelry - Little or none. Conservative watch. No earrings.
- Aftershave - Minimal. Light or nothing at all.
- Hairstyle - Neat, professional
- Nails - Trimmed and clean
- Facial hair - Groomed
- Portfolio/briefcase

What Not to Bring

- Gum
- Cell phone - Turn completely off
- iPod or any other electronic device*
- Piercings - Leave at home and only wear earrings if possible
- Tattoos - Cover up as much as possible
- Backpacks - Use a padfolio** or briefcase instead
- Cleavage - Wear appropriate clothes
- See-through garments
- Coat - Give to the receptionist

* Unless it is needed in the interview.
** Leather bound folder that usually contains a writing pad.

Additional Tips

- Clothes
    - Make sure they fit, are clean, and well pressed
    - Prepare them the night before
    - Inspect for tags or dangling threads
    - No missing buttons
    - No lint
- Clean fingernails
- No dangling earrings or full arm bracelets
- Padfolio is preferred over a briefcase
- Bring an extra pair of panty hose
- Bring your Portfolio

A successful interview allows you to present a set of skills that equals or exceeds your competition, together with a conservative appearance. Dress like the situation demands and focus on being different from everyone else by using your communication skills to highlight your accomplishments.

Diet (Product Ingredients)

Wearing the right outfit and being attentive to the smallest details of your appearance conveys a sincere effort on your part to look your best on the outside. Do you place the same emphasis on what is going on inside? Apparently many in the U.S. don't as noted by the Centers for Disease Control and Prevention. According to their findings in the years spanning 2009-2010, 69.2% percent of adults, 20 years and older, qualify as being overweight and 35.9% are considered obese.

Being overweight can affect every facet of a person's life and be especially detrimental to your career as differences get noticed. Differences are beneficial for a product sitting on a shelf waiting to be noticed, but detrimental to the job seeker in the hiring process. As noted earlier, your appearance during an interview should support your overall message. Any variances outside of the norm can adversely affect your ability to reach your goals. What are the detrimental effects of being overweight? There are many, but for our purposes we'll focus on the three that have the greatest impact.

Promotability

Weight issues can hinder a person's ability to get hired and/or promoted. Due to the sagging economy, competition for jobs and promotions are fiercer than ever. While managers want to fill jobs with the right person, biases play a part in the process. This was reinforced in a study done at Yale that found 'Weight-ism' was more widespread than Racism. Biases regarding weight issues are now more prevalent than race or gender discrimination. While these types (gender, race, weight) differ significantly from each other, the effect is the same. It keeps worthy candidates from getting the jobs they deserve and want.

Earning Power

Obese Americans have smaller paychecks than those who aren't overweight. This difference is especially acute among women according to a study published in the Journal of Applied Psychology in fall 2010 titled, "When It Comes to Pay, Do the Thin Win?" It noted that:

- "Very thin" women earned approximately $22,000 more than their average-weight counterparts.

- "Thin" women earned a little over $7,000 more than their average-weight counterparts.

- "Heavy" and "Very Heavy" women lost over $9,000 and almost $19,000, respectively, more than their average-weight counterparts.

Project these disparities in compensation over a forty-year working career and a woman characterized as very thin would make over one and a half million dollars more than a woman characterized as very heavy.

Costs

There is a direct correlation in regard to medical costs and weight. Employers are keenly aware of the link between employees' health and the insurance premiums they pay. Because of this, employers have begun taking proactive measures. For example, a new policy recently enacted for employees of CVS Pharmacy requires them to report their weight, body fat and other health metrics — or they pay a fine that could add up to $600 each year.

What is pushing this issue to the forefront? Money! The annual healthcare cost of obesity in the U.S. has doubled in less than a decade and may be as high as $147 billion per year, says new government-sponsored research. The study was conducted by researchers at RTI International, the Agency for Healthcare Research and Quality, and the U.S. Centers for Disease Control and Prevention (CDC) and is published in the 27 July 2009 issue of the health policy journal *Health Affairs*.

Because health care costs are becoming a bigger and bigger expense, many employers are making concerted efforts to keep these costs as low as possible. To reduce current and future costs, employers have begun scrutinizing the risks imposed by:

> *New Hires* – In an effort to mitigate unnecessary risks, employers will try to avoid hiring people with issues such as excess weight, nicotine use, excessive alcohol use, etc.

> *Current Employees* – Are encouraged to utilize programs within and outside the organization such as wellness visits, discounts on gym memberships, counseling, etc. Employers are beginning to realize preventative approaches can cost a fraction compared to medical care.

To summarize, weight issues can have very unfavorable consequences regarding all aspects of a person's career. Small or seemingly inconsequential biases in hiring, pay, and insurance premiums play a role in decreasing earning power. The cumulative effect of these slights over an entire career, can have a profound effect on goals, earning power, and self-esteem.

If this is an issue that may affect you, be proactive by taking action now rather than later by checking out http://www.nutrition.gov/. Along with providing nutritional information, it has a section on weight management. Educate yourself on good eating habits and living a healthy lifestyle. Don't give someone discriminating power over you. Your career and bank account depend upon it.

Fitness (Product Durability)

How durable are you? If you are young, do you have the stamina to work 40+ years? If you are middle-age or older, do you have what it takes to make it to that finish line called retirement. Remaining fit is essential to reaching your goals and being productive over the long haul of a working life. We just highlighted the importance of proper nutrition and the role it can play in your career. We now look at the other important element, exercise.

Fitness is the foundation upon which a healthy life is predicated and acts as a deterrent to unhealthy behaviors. When done consistently, it spills over into all aspects of life by promoting:

- healthy eating habits
- a restful night's sleep
- a proper work life balance

If you have let this area of your life slide a bit or need some ideas on where to start, go to http://www.fitness.gov/. The federal government has issued its first-ever Physical Activity Guidelines for Americans. They describe the types and amounts of physical activity that offer substantial health benefits.

Price

The dilemma for any business is deciding on what price to charge for the goods they sell. If prices are too high, customers will go elsewhere. Set too low, profitability suffers and the business could fail. Because this is such an important issue, companies do a great deal of research trying to figure out the right price to charge. At a minimum, a business will normally look at two things before making that determination. First, what it costs to make the product or provide the service. Second, to find out what the competition charges for a similar product or service.

Let's look at a business common to almost every town that sells a universally liked product, pizza! How does the pizza shop know what prices to put on their menu? A good first step is calculating the costs needed to make each item on the menu. The expenses associated with making a plain pizza are the cost of the ingredients (dough, sauce, cheese, etc.). Knowing how much these items cost will provide a rough idea of what to charge. The second piece of information is knowing what the other shops in the area charge for a plain pizza. Taken together, these two pieces of information allow the pizza shop owner to make a more informed decision regarding what to charge for a plain pizza.

Similar to a business owner, you need to know how much to charge for your services. In other words, what level of compensation must an employer pay you to work at a particular job? You'll want to find an answer to that question as soon as possible because salary can be discussed at any time during the interview process. Asking for too little diminishes your earning power and may cause you to struggle to meet your financial obligations. Asking for too much may price yourself out of contention, not get the job, and put you into deeper financial straits. What's worse, not having a chance to get the job at all or getting the job but being under paid?

Smart businesses know all about their competition by carefully and consistently doing research. We suggest you do the same due diligence and find out what employers are paying for specific jobs. Several methods are available in acquiring this information and are noted below:

On-line

Obtaining in-depth information regarding all things associated with compensation is very easy through the use of the Internet. Sites such as Salary.com http://www.salary.com/, Payscale http://www.payscale.com/, and Glassdoor http://www.glassdoor.com/Salaries/index.htm provide a wealth of salary information for specific job titles in any geographic region of the country.

Job Boards

Sites like Monster http://monster.salary.com/, CareerBuilder http://www.cbsalary.com/, and Indeed http://www.indeed.com/salary aren't just for job postings. They can also provide you with a customized salary range based on your education, experience, and location.

Network

Do you know someone that works, or used to work, at a specific company? They can provide valuable information regarding non-advertised job openings, pay, benefits, working conditions, along with a foot in the door opportunity.

Temp/Staffing Agencies

These types of agencies are in the business of providing qualified, pre-screened temporary workers to employers. The positions they help fill are for a variety of different jobs, in varied settings, for short periods of time. Because of this, they have the pulse on the hiring needs of many employers along with intimate knowledge of the pay ranges of various jobs. While the positions are temporary, this type of work can provide a variety of experiences and in some cases lead to permanent employment.

Volunteer/Internships

Don't be afraid to give up some of your time in order to gain valuable information. These types of experiences allow you to find out about the inner workings of local companies, gain valuable experience, and build a group of networking contacts. Perhaps the most important reason - it is one of the best ways to obtain a job. In the National Association of Colleges & Employers (NACE) 2012 Internship & Co-op Survey it was reported that more than 40% of the total expected number of new hires for 2011 – 2012 were anticipated to come from a company's internship program.

School Counselor

While their focus is on providing academic guidance, counselors at various educational institutions often have contacts and relevant information regarding the local business community.

Career Services

Career schools, community colleges, and universities can provide a wealth of information and guidance. As a liaison between students and employers, the career services department's job is to help connect graduates with companies that need to fill employment openings.

Career Link (State agencies)

These state-affiliated agencies help connect unemployed and displaced workers with companies that are hiring. They provide a myriad of services to anyone seeking help with any part of the employment process. To find the agency for your state, go to http://www.statelocalgov.net/50states-jobs.cfm.

We highly recommend taking the time to research your local area to gain a sufficient understanding of the marketplace and what it has to offer. Not knowing your worth during salary negotiations gives the employer a distinct advantage. Missing out on being paid a percent or two more may seem inconsequential, but can lead to the loss of thousands of dollars over the span of our whole career. In the section on Selling later in this chapter, we show you just how much that difference can be. Therefore, educate yourself on industry standards regarding pay rates and benefits for your specialty. The more information you have, the better your position will be during negotiations, and the more likely you will be paid fairly for your work.

Place

There is an old saying about starting a business, "The three most important things in business are location, location, location." While that may be an oversimplification, place often plays a critical role in the success or failure of a business. To put place in the proper context and how it fits into the product mix, we go back to our pizza shop example. We have already looked at the importance of providing a quality product at a competitive price. Now we have to decide where to make and sell our product. What is the best location for the pizza shop? Next to another pizza shop? Probably not! Questions to ask in helping find the right location might be:

> How many pizza shops are within a 10-mile radius?

> What is the population needed to support one pizza shop?

> What are the demographics (age, gender, education level, home ownership, etc.) of a particular area?

> Which segment of this population is most likely to order pizza?

Knowing this information helps a business make more informed decisions.

Location must be a consideration in regards to where you will work. Maybe it's the area where you have lived all your life and the one in which you have strong ties to family, friends, children, etc. Or, perhaps you are willing to relocate anywhere to land that perfect job. Regardless, it's a good idea to reassess from time to time whether the place you currently choose to live is the best place to achieve your professional goals. Where you ultimately decide to work – urban, suburban, rural –will have an impact on your employment opportunities and earning potential. Below we briefly describe the characteristics of these areas:

Urban Areas

Urban areas are characterized by a high density of businesses and people. This density creates a variety of employment opportunities and on average pay higher wages than any of the other areas discussed below. However, these higher wages lead to a very competitive job market and greater cost of living, especially the costs associated with housing, and food.

Suburban Areas

Suburban areas are where a large portion of the urban workers live. While business density is lower than an urban center, these areas provide ample job opportunities due to the needs of the local population. While salaries on average may not be as high as the urban centers, this is often offset by lower living costs.

Rural Areas

Rural areas, or the country, have a low population density with large areas devoted to agriculture. While the cost of living can be the lowest in these areas, employment opportunities are fewer and wages are normally the lowest compared to other areas.

What should you do? Like the pizza shop, you'll have to do some research in determining the best place to live and work. Answering fundamental questions like, "Can I get a job that I like, pays well, and has a promising future where I currently live?" is a good place to start. If not, what are your options?

> **Get more education?** Are there specific industries and employers in your area that require particular types of education and training you do not have? Check out the schools in your area and follow our recommendations in Chapter 3.

> **Settle for what the area has to offer?** This may not seem like a big deal now but could lead to regrets later in life if you feel your skills, abilities, and interests were never pursued. Assess your options to see if your goals can be reached where you currently reside.

> **Move?** Don't be afraid to relocate, if necessary! It's okay to realize you may not be able to maximize your opportunities and fulfill your dreams and desires where you grew up or are currently located. The realization that the area where you currently reside does not have the best prospects to make a good living can be difficult to accept. A little perspective regarding this issue may help. Throughout time, individuals from around the world have relocated in order to make a living wage. These migrations have been for various reasons such as political and social unrest, environmental disasters, and economic turmoil. This is natural part of a continuous cycle requiring many to make difficult choices.

Ultimately, it requires a balance between the known and unknown. Should you stay in an area that may only provide limited opportunities for success or move to an area that may have more favorable circumstances? This can be a tough choice, especially if you have to leave behind your family and everything you know. What can help with this process? The Internet. It allows you to look for jobs in any part of the country, or even the world for that matter. Look at employments ads in your field of interest, from all over the country. Are there areas where jobs are more plentiful? Pay more? What does the area have to offer in terms of housing, entertainment, education? Finding out more information about an area, will provide insight, offer a better perspective, and allow you to make a more informed decision.

Promotion

We now look at the last, and arguably most important, P in the marketing mix, promotion. As noted in the beginning of this chapter, every company must attract, inform, and persuade potential customers to buy their products and services. This requires the use of advertising and often can be one of the larger expenses in a business's budget.

Because advertising can be very expensive, successful companies closely track their marketing efforts in order to gauge effectiveness. The methods that bring in customers are continued while methods that don't appear to work are discontinued or changed. Similarly, you will need to make these same types of decisions as you look for a job.

Searching for a job may require contacting, interacting, and following up with a large number of people. Therefore, you'll want a system that helps you keep track of all this valuable information. We have devoted the first part of this section to the organizational aspects of looking for a job. We conclude the chapter by looking at the various ways in which you can promote yourself in the most effective ways possible.

Tracking Prospects (Inventory)

Successful businesses manage two types of inventory well, products and people. The first is what most of us associate with when we hear the word inventory. Namely, the storage of materials used in making a product. The second kind, and less well-known, is about managing customers. Because they are the lifeblood of any business, companies spend a great deal of time and money tracking and analyzing customers and potential prospects. To do this effectively and efficiently, software called Customer Relationship Management (CRM) is utilized. CRMs provide in-depth information about the customer (who's buying, who's not, how much they buy, when, how often, etc.). Analyzing this data allows a company to focus its attention on those people who are most to likely buy from them.

Do you know which companies to focus your attention on? You'll need to find out, in order not to waste your time and efforts on those companies that won't and can't hire you. To do so, you'll need to build your own inventory of prospects. It doesn't have to be elaborate or complicated but it should help you answer the following questions:

- What companies are located in my area?
- Do they have a website?
- Type of business (what do they do?)
- Relevant jobs (Are there jobs applicable to my education and experience?)
- Who is the contact person regarding hiring?
- What is the contact information?
- Date(s) contacted?

A good tool to use for this purpose is a spreadsheet program like Excel or Google Docs www.docs.google.com. An example of how your spreadsheet can be set up is shown below in Figure 6.1:

Figure 6.1 – Prospect Inventory

Company Name	Website	Type of Business	Relevant Jobs	Contact Person	Contact Information	Contact Date(s)

Enter the data you have collected from your networking activities. Also, complement this information with your own investigative work by researching as many companies as possible in the area where you live, or want to live. The Internet can provide a wealth of data in a short period of time. When you have collected some data, put it to good use by following the steps listed below:

1. Write a cover letter to accompany your resume to each company on the list. Refer back to Chapter 5 (Communication) if you need help constructing a proper cover letter. Because you are applying to different companies, your letter needs to be different as well. Use your uniqueness to write a cover letter that will help separate you from the competition.

2. Mail your cover letter and resume via regular mail. I know what you are thinking. Nobody does that anymore due to email and on-line applications. That may be true but is precisely why you want to take the road less traveled. Playing by the rules hinders your ability to stand out from the competition.

    Businesses still use this form of communication to get customers and it can work for you. If you also applied on-line, make sure you mention this in your cover letter if applicable. Remember, it's not about the quantity of letters you mail but the quality. If you take the time to do thorough research, it should produce quality leads for you to pursue.

3. First follow-up - Send your cover letter and resume via email to everyone who has not responded to your first mailing. You can do this two ways:

    - Copy your cover letter into the email and attach your resume. Include a link to your LinkedIn account https://www.linkedin.com/ under your signature.

    - Attach your resume and cover letter to the email and write a brief note.

    Wait a week, two at the most before following up. If you don't hear anything, go to Step 4.

4. Second follow-up - Pick up the phone and call. Your cover letter and resume have already introduced you to the company. Your call can be as simple as an inquiry to see if they received your information. You may:

- Have difficulty even speaking to anyone.
- Just get an acknowledgment your information was received.
- Actually get to speak to the person your letter was addressed to. This should be your goal and is the goal of every salesperson. Having a few minutes with the decision-maker may not land you a job but it certainly helps you get recognized for future opportunities.

I know what you are thinking; this is a lot of work. As we'll see shortly, this type of work can pay big dividends by allowing you to find those hidden jobs the public never sees. By doing the steps listed above, you begin to tap into opportunities before anyone else. The quote, "timing is everything," applies here. Once a job is posted, you may be competing with thousands of other job seekers. Your ability to stand out from the crowd can be difficult. Whereas applying before, or right when, a job opens up can put you at the front of the line.

By going through this process, you'll probably get the following:

- No response
- We are not hiring at the moment
- We only accept applications on-line. Many companies may still ask you to complete an on-line application as part of their formal hiring process. That's okay. Making contact with a company in different ways can only help get you noticed.
- A phone call or email to schedule an interview.

You'll likely get many more negative rather than positive responses. That is to be expected and is part of any sales process. Good salesmen will tell you to get the no's out of the way so you can find the companies that will say yes. We discuss what you need to do when you get a yes in the section below on managing the process.

Active Marketing

What strategies will you use to connect to employers that are hiring? More specifically, how will you connect to those companies that are hiring *and* have openings that align with your education and experience? That is your target market (best customers) and where you must focus your efforts. To reach your best customers, you'll need to do two types of marketing, active and passive.

Promotional activities that require effort on your part, are deliberate, and done on a consistent basis are considered active marketing. We recommend you incorporate all of the following active marketing methods into your job search:

Networking

Businesses consistently rank networking as their number one marketing method. Why? Because people like to do business with someone they know. The same applies in the hiring process. Per Randall S. Hansen, Ph.D. of www.quintcareers.com "Only about 15-20 percent of all available jobs are ever publicly advertised in any medium (newspapers, on-line, etc.). The vast majority of job openings are part of the "hidden" or "closed" job market. And the higher the position and salary, the less likely the position will be advertised at all." Just like a business, you'll need to incorporate networking into your routine to discover those hidden jobs.

In most cases, employers would rather take a short cut in the hiring process and hire someone they know. Referred and recommended candidates greatly lessen the time and expense associated with filling a vacant position. Because recommendations and referrals carry such great weight in the hiring process, it is incumbent that you develop your own network of contacts.

Your options regarding networking are many. Below we break it down further into two major categories – on-line and in-person – and the best way to take advantage of each.

On-line Networking

On-line networking utilizes the power of social media to connect and interact with others. Below we look at a few of the more popular platforms.

- ➢ LinkedIn www.LinkedIn.com is by far the largest networking site for interacting and communicating with other professionals. Setting up your own profile is easy and allows you to connect with past and present co-workers along with industry experts. It is a community of users that can help you:

- ❖ Find a job.
- ❖ Connect with peers and industry leaders.
- ❖ Find business opportunities.
- ❖ Research companies.

Because this information may be viewed by many, especially potential employers, take the time to make your profile as accurate and complete as possible. Need help setting it up? Check out http://www.wikihow.com/Create-an-Account-on-LinkedIn for more information.

➢ Facebook www.facebook.com is the largest networking site on the planet. While mainly known as a vehicle to share personal information between users, it is increasingly being used as a professional networking tool as well. However, caution is urged. Unlike LinkedIn, Facebook is generally skewed much more toward social usage rather than for professional purposes. Therefore, if you are going to actively promote yourself using this site, we suggest:

- ❖ Carefully choosing who you associate with, as your profile can be viewed by all your friends and by their friends.
- ❖ Looking at your profile. Would it discourage someone from hiring you based on the information they see?
- ❖ Making your profile as uncluttered and simple as possible by minimizing graphics and widgets.
- ❖ Limiting content to information relevant to your career and to your job search efforts.

➢ Twitter https://twitter.com/ is altering the way in which we communicate. A service that allows users to send and read texts messages (tweets) up to 140 characters in length, it is rapidly becoming a way to follow industry leaders. Per Dan Finnigan, CEO of Jobvite, "34% of job seekers said they were using Twitter to find work, and he is convinced that percentage will continue to expand." To use it effectively:

- ❖ Maintain two accounts, one for personal and one for professional use.

❖ Keep your information (picture and bio) up to date.
❖ Start following people and companies that can help you. Use the "what to follow tab" for help.
❖ Be active by creating new content, retweeting articles, asking questions, and sending notes to people you are following. It's not the number of relationships you develop but the quality of each that will help you in the long run.

On-line social networking is a great way to create powerful profiles that uniquely describe your best attributes, skill sets, education, and experience. This is important because employers are increasingly using the Internet to find as much information as possible about potential candidates. If a candidate utilizes social networking, their LinkedIn, Facebook, Twitter, and other on-line profiles, often show up first or very high in these searches. This is because search engines give a great deal of weight to information that is either new or recent. It also pushes irrelevant, or less flattering, information further down the search results page.

In-Person Networking

In-person networking uses the power of face-to-face meetings to develop and strengthen lasting relationships. Will you know what to say once you get in front of people that can help your career? A prepared elevator speech can help and allows you to quickly convey your value to others. Because this is an essential element on your quest for the perfect job, you should spend some time developing the right pitch. We look at the most effective ways to accomplish this before considering the various networking situations that are available.

> **Elevator Speech** - Per Wikipedia, "An elevator pitch, elevator speech, or elevator statement is a short summary used to quickly and simply define a person, profession, product, service, organization or event and its value proposition.
>
> The name "elevator pitch" reflects the idea that it should be possible to deliver the summary in the time span of an elevator ride, or approximately thirty seconds to two minutes. The term itself comes

from a scenario of an accidental meeting with someone important in the elevator. If the conversation inside the elevator in those few seconds is interesting and value adding, the conversation will continue after the elevator ride or end in an exchange of business cards or a scheduled meeting."

All the work you put into your resume, portfolio, and cover letters will be for naught unless you can verbalize this information in a 15-30 second advertisement that genuinely describes you. Nancy Collamer of www.NextAvenue.org, provides a practical way to do this. She says, "A good pitch should answer three questions: Who are you? What do you do? What are you looking for?"

We'll use her suggestion, and the color-coded technique used previously to create an objective statement for your resume from Chapter 1, to assist you in developing a memorable elevator speech.

- Who are you?
- *What do you do?*
- What are you looking for?
- Extras – If you additional time, elaborate on any special skills you may have.

Below are several examples of elevator speeches that reflect the various stages in a jobseeker's career:

Figure 6.2 – Elevator Speech (High School Graduate)

Hi, I am Jane J. Jobseeker, *a high school graduate*, and am looking for a position in the IT industry. I am particularly adept at creating informative websites that get noticed by customers.

> *Figure 6.3 – Elevator Speech (College Graduate Without Paid Work Experience)*

Hi, I am Jane J. Jobseeker, *a college graduate*, and am looking for a position in accounting. My course work in college, along with an internship at ABC Accounting, has allowed me to gain experience in QuickBooks and Peachtree software programs.

> *Figure 6.4 – Elevator Speech (College Graduate With Paid Work Experience)*

Hi, I am Jane J. Jobseeker, *an executive assistant with a proven record of cost-saving initiatives*, and am seeking a management position in a small to mid-sized company. I am particularly adept at finding ways to make things run smoother, more efficiently, and less expensively.

You've taken the time to highlight your achievements on paper, take the next step and put it into words. Place yourself in situations where you can practice saying it. When it doesn't sound like a commercial, you'll know you are on the right track. Below are some ways to spread the word about you:

- **Family and friends** - The most common advice given to budding entrepreneurs (new business owners) is to tell as many people as possible about the venture. First on that list should be friends and family given the relative ease in spreading the word. The same logic should be used in your approach to finding a job. Let everyone know you are looking for a job and the particular types of jobs you are interested in. This allows many people, with your best interest at heart, to be on the lookout for opportunities.

- **Connections** –The three big R's (relationships, referrals, and recommendations) are all about making connections. These can help you gain a decided advantage in your job search. Do you know someone at a company you would like to work for? Do you know someone that knows the hiring manager? If so, use these individuals to help get your foot in the door. At the very least, find as much as you can about the business and its culture. What do they value? Who is their ideal candidate? Use this information to help connect you with the company you want to work for.

- **Recommendations** – Nothing is quite as powerful as a recommendation. These types of endorsements help build your profile and describe your accomplishments in a unique way. Businesses use them daily to help sell products and services. You too can easily give and receive recommendations by using social networking sites like LinkedIn. One of the easiest ways to get a recommendation is to write one for a current or former colleague. Most likely, they will return the favor and write one on your behalf. To be really effective, the person writing the recommendation should be as detailed, descriptive, and accurate as possible. Endorsements will further add to the narrative about who you really are.

- **Co-workers** – J.T. O'Donnell, founder of the on-line career website www.careerealism.com neatly puts work into perspective when she says, "Every job is temporary." Because of this, it's imperative you maintain a friendly and professional relationship with as many people as possible. These connections lay the foundation of your professional network and provide opportunities for future collaborations, recommendations, and references.

- **Groups** – A great way to meet, and get to know, people is by joining or participating in group activities. While not everyone you meet can help get you a job, they may know someone who can. Therefore, you'll want to put yourself in places that provide opportunities to interact and connect with a variety of different individuals. A great way to expand your reach and meet new contacts is by:

    - Volunteering for local nonprofits and charities.
    - Joining civic groups such as the Lions Club, Rotary, and Kiwanis.
    - Being active in professional associations relevant to the industry in which you are working or wish to work in.
    - Participating in the alumni association(s) of all the schools you attended.

Networking groups, like friendships, need consistent attention, continuous nurturing, and constant infusion of new people. Therefore, participation in professional and personal networking events is crucial in developing relationships in the present that may be able to help you in the future.

➤ **Door-to-Door (Canvassing)** – Due to the backlash in telemarketing and the high costs of direct mail, many businesses use canvassing to get in front of the customer. Canvassing involves walking/driving to various businesses and either speaking with the manager or dropping off literature. In the case of the pizza business, it may involve handing out menus in a particular area. This type of activity, while time intensive, can help find jobs that will never be advertised and allow the right person at the right time to get hired. While this is not the normal method of distributing your resume in the age of the Internet, it can get you noticed by the hiring manager or even the owner.

When using this approach, we recommend being ready for anything. Good salespeople fully prepare for all contingencies when visiting a prospective client and you have to do the same. Therefore, you will need to:

- Have your elevator speech, discussed previously, polished and ready to go.
- Dress professionally.
- Be ready for an interview at a moment's notice.
- Discuss salary if this topic is broached.

Just like in sales, you also have to realize you may be turned away from many more places than welcomed. Many companies do this because:

- They may not be hiring.
- Their application process starts on-line.
- They may discourage solicitation of any kind.

Regardless of the outcome of your visits, try and gather information that will help in your job search. If possible:

- ❖ Obtain the business card of the hiring manager.
- ❖ Find out if the company is hiring.
- ❖ Verify the steps in the company's hiring process.
- ❖ Ask for referrals. If they aren't hiring, do they know of anybody else who is?

➢ **Job (Career) fairs** - Many businesses make trade shows or conventions an integral part of their marketing efforts to get in front of potential customers. This type of venue, in which many different companies gather to show off their products and services, can bring many customers and companies together in a short period of time.

Job or Career Fairs use a similar model and are an ideal way to draw a large number of quality candidates in one place. Many colleges, as well as employment agencies, often sponsor these types of events to help graduates and job seekers find employment.

If you haven't already done so, you'll want to incorporate these into your marketing plan and attend as many as possible. Like all your other marketing activities, proper preparation is the key to success. What you need to do, before, during, and after attending a job fair is discussed below:

Before

Even though there may be hundreds, if not thousands of job seekers attending, you still must prepare the same way as if you were going on a typical interview. Therefore, you will want to:

➢ Find out the **companies** that are going to be in attendance. Make a list of those you absolutely want to speak with. If you have extra time, speak with as many people and companies as possible.

➢ Know something about each company by doing **research**. At a minimum, review their website. You may get an interview on the spot and just knowing some basic company information can be very valuable.

- Finalize your **resume**. If you are applying for different types of jobs, modify your resume where necessary to make it applicable for each position.

- Bring a **padfolio/portfolio** to hold your resumes, take notes and store any literature you may receive from various companies.

- Practice your **elevator speech**. This topic was previously discussed above in the section titled In-Person Networking.

During

- Be appropriately **dressed.** If necessary, review the section on product in this chapter regarding appearance.

- **Arrive** early. Because the economy has been stubborn to fully recover, you'll probably have plenty of company as there is approximately 1 job for every 3 jobseekers.

- If you find yourself standing in line, **network** with those around you. You'll be surprised what can be learned about the companies in attendance or about other opportunities.

- Be **enthusiastic**. Company recruiters are keenly aware of the attitude and body language of job seekers and can spot insincerity a mile away. Therefore, come with a smile, be eager, and show some excitement.

- **Treat** everyone you meet like it is an interview. That means with a firm handshake, eye contact, and attentive listening.

- Ask **questions** but not those that are obvious. If the answer to a question you asked can be found on the company website, it shows a lack of poor preparation on your part.

After

- Get the **contact information** from every company representative you speak with. An easy way to do this is by collecting business cards.

- **Enter** this information into your spreadsheet shown above.

- Follow-up in writing as soon as possible. Below is an example:

    "It was a pleasure meeting you at the xyz job fair. I am very interested in pursuing employment with your company, especially after hearing more about the various opportunities available."

- Increase your networking contacts by inviting your new acquaintances to **connect** with you via LinkedIn.

- If they are unable to offer you employment at this time, ask for a **referral.** Can they put you in touch with someone who may be able to further your career objectives?

- Think of these types of activities as **practice.** The more comfortable you become speaking with employers, the greater your chances will be of getting hired in the future.

Passive Marketing

Passive marketing involves strategic placement of your information in places where companies can find out more about you. For example, it could be an employer who finds your resume or profile on-line and contacts you for an interview. Because your information is accessible 24/7, it's always working for you. Below are some passive marketing methods you'll want to incorporate into your job search:

Website

To be seen as legitimate, a business needs to have a website. It allows potential customers the ability to research product and service offerings including pertinent historical and background information. In other words, it allows the visitor to get introduced to the company on their terms and their time. The website can play a key part in the *attract, inform, persuade* segment of the sales process.

Have you thought about posting your information on-line? It's like a billboard saying, "Here are my credentials, come and get me." While there is some concern regarding privacy issues, it is dynamic, can easily be changed, and shows your willingness to utilize and embrace technology. Need help putting your information on-line, refer back to Chapter 1 (Your Resume) specifically, Step 5 (Distribution Methods) for more information.

Job Boards

Most, if not all, the major job boards – Monster, CareerBuilder, Indeed, and SimplyHired – allow jobseekers to upload a resume for free. However, they don't do this because of purely altruistic reasons. These sites make their money by allowing employers to comb through their large database of resumes in exchange for a fee. Because of this, your resume may be viewed by many different employers. While the success obtained with this type of promotion is limited, it can provide you with the ability to receive alerts regarding job postings which may be of interest.

Networking Sites

Reviewed earlier in this section, sites like LinkedIn, Twitter, and Facebook are changing the way people communicate and that includes looking for a job. Incorporate some, or all, of these methods in your job search depending upon your comfort level.

Although this type of marketing does not require nearly as much attention as active marketing, it still requires some due diligence on your part. Periodically, you'll need to make sure your billboard reflects your most recent credentials. To keep your profiles properly updated, make changes when:

- Your job status changes. Did you get:
    - A promotion?
    - A new job title?
    - New responsibilities?
- You change employers.
- Your status changes (full-time to part-time and vice versa).
- You receive new certifications.
- You have obtained another educational degree.
- There are changes you feel more accurately represent your current situation.

Changes made to your on-line profile(s) get more attention as web crawlers (information gathering devices on the Internet) are attracted to new information. At a minimum, make a conscious effort to look at your on-line profiles and resume at least every three to six months and update where necessary.

Managing the Process - *The Sales Pipeline*

As you can see, it takes a great deal of work, preparation, and discipline to get a job but is made easier when approached in an organized way. In this section, we continue to build on that theme by developing a system to help you track the entire employment process. The steps in this process are noted below:

1. Cover Letter
2. Resume
3. Job Application
4. Employer Screening
5. Employer Testing
6. Interview
7. Negotiations

If you have followed our recommendations, your marketing efforts should begin to generate leads (interest from employers). Because each lead has the possibility of turning into a significant opportunity, it's important for you to keep track of every one. Great companies do this by setting up a system commonly referred to as a Sales Pipeline. This is a systematic approach to selling products and services in the most efficient way possible. Done correctly, it tracks potential customers from the first point of contact all the way through the various stages of the sales process. Increasingly, many companies are using a CRM, discussed earlier, to help manage this information.

Visually, a sales campaign looks something like figure 6.5. In the beginning, many people or companies are considered potential customers (suspects) depending on whether they react to various marketing activities. Suspects that don't react are removed from the list of potential customers narrowing the lead pool. As the lead pool narrows so does the funnel, as shown in Figure 6.5, along with the pool of prospects (those most likely to buy the product or service offerings). While it may seem like a game of attrition (loss of people or businesses), it's really just bringing into focus a smaller subset of likely customers. This yields a savings of time and energy by focusing only on those prospects who will buy and not on those who won't or can't buy.

**Figure 6.5
Sales Pipeline**

Your mission is the same. You must focus exclusively on those companies which can or will hire you rather than the ones which can't or won't. To be successful in your endeavor, you'll need a system to track your prospects (companies that will hire you). We outline the actions needed to accomplish this by looking at each step in the employment process.

Steps 1 and 2: (Cover Letter and Resume)

Due to the prominent status placed on the resume and cover letter, it is worth restating an important point made in Chapter 5 (Communication). Both must be unique for each position you intend to apply for and modified accordingly. Your guide in making them distinct is the job posting. Read it several times to get the true feel of what the position entails and the kind of person the company is searching for. When you have a better grasp of the job, incorporate some key words from the posting into your resume and cover letter. This extra work pays off and aligns your cover letter, resume, and job description into a complete narrative.

After taking the time to carefully apply to specific job postings, it's crucial you be able to easily access this information. It can be done either manually or electronically depending on your comfort level.

Manually

Print your resume, cover letter, and a copy of the job posting and place them in a paper file folder. Maintain separate folders for each employer and log the important dates on the inside front or back cover of each folder. See the example in figure 6.6 below. Place the folders in alphabetical order by company name to ensure quick access.

Figure 6.6 – Action Log

Date	Event
11/12/13	Resume and cover letter submitted
11/16/13	1st follow-up call made
11/23/13	1st telephone interview
11/25/13	1st in-person interview

Electronically

Follow the same procedures as noted under the manual method but utilize the electronic folders on your computer to store documents. Create a main folder titled Job Search. Within that folder, set up folders for each employer you sent a resume or completed application. Figure 6.7 below shows what it looks like graphically:

Figure 6.7 – Job Search File Organizer

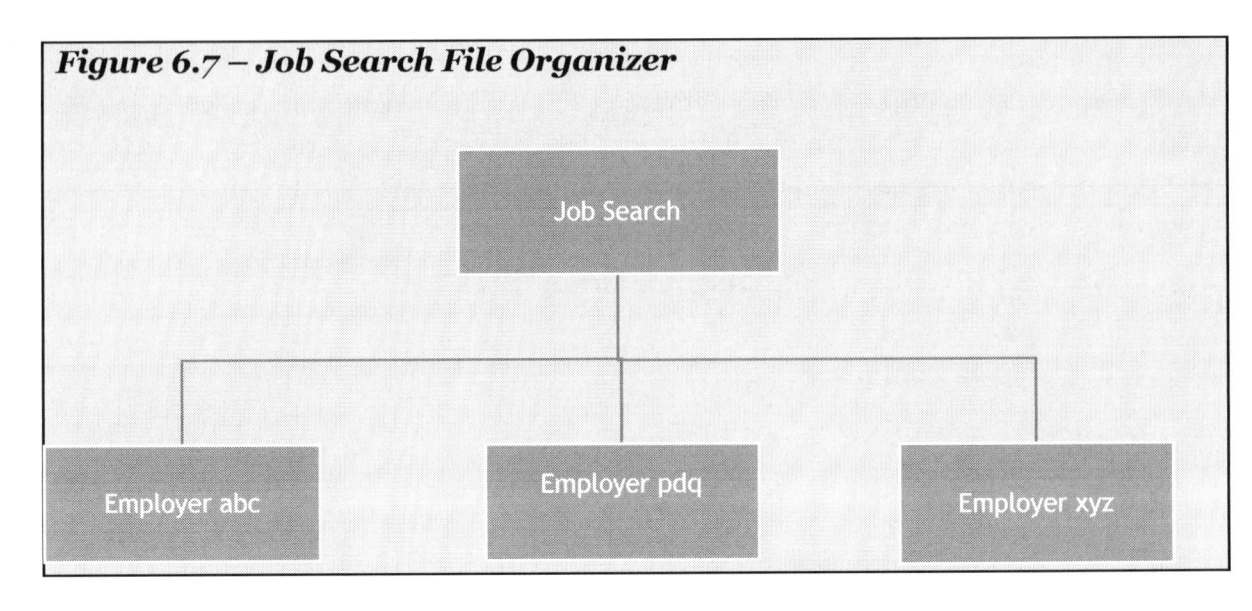

```
                    Job Search
                   /     |     \
        Employer abc  Employer pdq  Employer xyz
```

Inside each employer file should contain a copy of:

- your cover letter
- your resume
- the job description

The above will be documents you modified or completed for a specific job. When saving, use a naming convention that describes the document, company, and position applied for. An example of this would be **cover letter-abc-admin-assist.doc**. Also, use these folders to save your research along with any correspondence between you and the employer.

Setting up this type of an organizational structure may seem like a lot of work. However, it will allow you to:

- Be better prepared for future interactions with prospective employers.
- Know exactly what job the employer is contacting you about.
- Be looking at the same documents as the interviewer eliminating confusion and surprises.

Previously, we showed how potential employers can be tracked using a spreadsheet as shown in Figure 6.1 above. We recommend expanding this spreadsheet to include additional columns related to your job search as shown in

Figure 6.8 below. Carefully tracking your efforts will indicate the current status of each job and where to focus your energies. Don't waste your time on employers who do not respond after several attempts. Focus your time on other prospects.

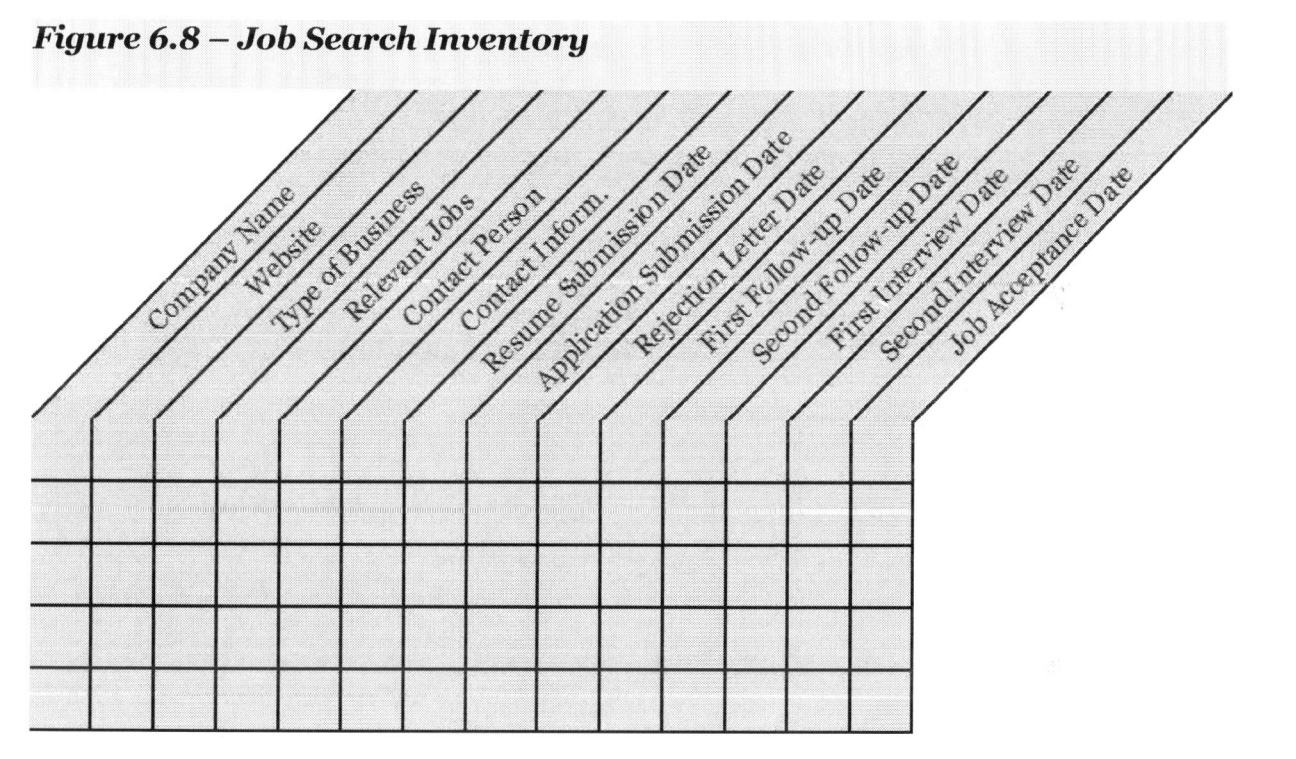

Figure 6.8 – Job Search Inventory

Columns: Company Name, Website, Type of Business, Relevant Jobs, Contact Person, Contact Inform., Resume Submission Date, Application Submission Date, Rejection Letter Date, First Follow-up Date, Second Follow-up Date, First Interview Date, Second Interview Date, Job Acceptance Date

Step 3: (Job Application)

After the resume and cover letter, the next hurdle placed before every candidate is the job application. It too must be completed correctly in order to move to the next stage of the hiring process. Employers use the application to pre-screen/pre-qualify candidates, streamline the hiring process, and to provide a more complete story of the applicant. While the application format differs from company to company, they all generally consist of five major parts:

1. Personal Information
2. Education

3. Employment History
4. Position Applied For
5. References

Increasingly, employers are relying on technology to gather information about their applicants by making them apply on-line. While this information is mainly used as a screening tool, it also helps employers prove compliance with a variety of state and federal laws. Regardless of the format (paper or electronic) care should be taken when completing the application. Therefore, we recommend the following tips:

- Dress properly if completing in person.
- Read and follow all directions.
- Use black or blue ink pen if completing a paper application.
- Complete everything. Use N/A or Does Not Apply if the question is not applicable to you.
- Do not answer with statements like "same as above", or "see below".
- Neatness counts. Therefore, take your time.
- No spelling or grammatical errors.
- Use print rather than cursive writing.
- Be honest. You can be fined and/or fired for not telling the truth.
- Bring a fact sheet along to make the application process easier and faster. It should contain:
    - ❖ Employment history (Names, addresses, phone number, email address, beginning and ending dates, immediate supervisor, along with your starting and ending pay) of at least the last three employers, if applicable.
    - ❖ Volunteer work (Names, addresses, phone number, email address, beginning and ending dates, immediate supervisor and/or volunteer coordinator).

- ❖ References (Name, employer, if applicable, address, phone number, email address) of a mix (personal and professional) of at least 3 people.

- ❖ Your social security number.

➢ For on-line applications, consider printing out the form, complete it by hand, and then enter the information on-line when you have completed everything on the printed version.

➢ Check for completeness.

➢ Explain any gaps in your work history or education.

➢ No crossed out writing.

➢ Apply for a specific position.

➢ Sign and date the form.

➢ Treat the receptionist/assistant like gold.

➢ If you have been convicted of a felony or driving offense, fired, forced to resign, etc. have a good explanation of what happened.

➢ Resume and Cover Letter. Make sure they are readily available as many companies request these items at the same time an application is completed.

Remember, keep track of every application you filled out by noting the company name, date submitted, and the job title you applied for. Add this information to your job search database.

Step 4: (Employer Screening)

Per the Harvard Business Review, "80% of employee turnover is due to bad hiring decisions." Is it any wonder why a great deal of time, money, and resources, are spent in finding the right people? It's because hiring the wrong person can create huge disruptions that costs companies a great deal of money. Below we look at ways companies minimize this risk by examining the types of screening you may be subjected to in your job search.

Background Checks

Google, Facebook, LinkedIn, and Twitter, provide the means for employers to easily check the background of you and other potential candidates. Due to the relative ease in obtaining this information, it's often the first type of screening to be completed by an employer. The prevalence of this practice was recently confirmed by CareerBuilder, an on-line employment website, who found that 37% of hiring managers use social networking sites to research job applicants, with over 65% of that group using Facebook as their primary resource. To eliminate any surprises, we recommend you do a search of your name on the sites listed above, on all major search engines, along with any other sites you may visit regularly. Taking a proactive approach will allow you to:

Did you know?
53% of job applicants falsify information on their resume.
Source: Statistic Brain

- Be better prepared to discuss, with an interviewer, any information that may be unflattering or compromises your credibility.

- Review social networking sites you may belong to and remove any information that could hinder your chances of employment.

- Create on-line profiles with content that accurately reflect your professional and educational accomplishments. Setting up, and managing, a LinkedIn www.LinkedIn.com profile is a great way to begin this process and allows you to control content relative to your career.

While on-line searches may provide information about an applicant's social life, contacts, and other pieces of information, it often doesn't give the employer the complete picture of the job seeker. Therefore, prudent employers use other sources in trying to hire the right person and more importantly avoid hiring the wrong person. They most likely will:

- Contact previous employers.
- Request official transcripts from any educational institutions you attended.
- Contact some, or all, of the references you provided.

Your only job at this point is to provide complete and accurate information on your resume, cover letter, and application. Unfortunately, many job seekers are less than truthful regarding the information they provide. Per the Monster Hiring Resource Center, the top five lies told by job applicants are:

1. Exaggerating dates of past employment
2. Falsifying the degree or credentials earned
3. Inflating salary or title
4. Concealing a criminal record
5. Hiding a drug habit

It can be tempting to fib or exaggerate your credentials or try to hide a blemish from your past. Don't do it as the odds of getting caught have increased greatly through the use of technology. Instead, think about any items that may raise red flags and be ready with an explanation.

Criminal Background Checks

In the past, criminal background checks were largely used by schools, health care providers, and other public institutions to protect the safety of those they serve. This is now becoming standard practice for many employers due to the damages and liability that can be caused by an employee. For less than $20, employers can request information that will show an applicant's criminal, employment, educational, driving, and financial records. These are normally obtained from the state in which the applicant resides.

Employee Credit Reports

Whether this practice seems reasonable or not, credit reports are increasingly being used to determine your eligibility for employment. The credit report provides an overview of any debt you may have along with the payments made on that debt. Specifically, they provide a detailed listing of your payment history (loans, mortgages, and credit-card accounts) as well as any delinquencies, bankruptcies, judgments, and liens against you. The good news, before an employer can look at your credit history, they must have permission from you in writing. Also, you must be shown the report if you are rejected for a job due to your credit history.

Fairly or unfairly, employers use this information to help judge the character and integrity of a person. Many contend that an applicant with poor credit history may be unable to properly handle personal finance issues and be a sign of irresponsibility. These are just some of the questions that go through the mind of hiring professionals during this process. What can you do?

- ➢ Be proactive by reviewing your credit report regularly. Requesting your report is easier than ever and is discussed in Chapter 4 (Your Personal Finances).

- ➢ Review your report and check for mistakes.

- ➢ Be candid with the interviewer. A poor credit history can happen for a variety of reasons that are out of your control. Just be honest.

Employee credit checks are a trend that appears to be on the rise and was recently confirmed by the Society of Human Resource Management who said that 60% of employers run credit checks on all or some potential new hires. The good news, credit history ranked lowest among the criteria employers used to appraise candidates. Regardless, make sure you are up to date on your credit report history.

Step 5: (Employee Testing)

Employee testing takes many forms, varies with each employer, and is completed at different times in the hiring process. Below we look at some of the most common tests you may encounter:

Aptitude

Aptitude tests are used as a predictor of success in measuring an applicant's ability to perform various work-related activities. Some of the more popular types of tests measure abstract, verbal, numerical, spatial, and mechanical reasoning. However, the majority of the time they are used in determining reading comprehension, math level, and critical thinking skills. Many colleges and universities use these types of tests (Scholastic Aptitude Test – SAT, American College Testing – ACT) to measure the readiness of incoming students. Various industries and companies have also designed their own tests to measure specific job knowledge and whether a person is deemed a good fit for a particular job.

Skills

Skills tests measure an applicant's knowledge regarding specific abilities and whether they possess the minimum level necessary to excel at a particular job classification. The format of these tests can vary widely and range from words typed per minute to blueprint reading.

Integrity (honesty)

Honesty testing is often done at the beginning of the application process and is used primarily as a screening tool for candidates. Specifically, they are used to identify candidates who may be prone to high rates of absenteeism and disciplinary problems usually related to behaviors that are unproductive, risky, and dangerous.

Drug Screening

Used to detect the presence of drugs or alcohol, these tests try to eliminate candidates who may participate in risky behaviors. Depending on the industry or job, these tests may be required due to safety and performance reasons.

Physical Fitness

If a job requires a variety of physical movements, you may encounter pre-employment screening tests to measure physical fitness and whether you are able to fulfill the demands of the job. Candidates can be expected to do a variety of activities that assess endurance (muscular and cardiovascular) flexibility and strength that are often needed in certain types of jobs.

Personality

When assessing candidates, employers want to make sure they:

- Have the necessary skills.
- Have enthusiasm.
- Fit into the organization's culture.

The first two items, skills and enthusiasm, can often be determined through the normal course of the interview process (resume, cover letter, interview, references, etc.). When it comes to the organizational fit of a particular candidate, personality tests can help. Unlike an aptitude test, there is no right or wrong answer but measure a candidate's reaction across a wide spectrum of situations. Some employers analyze the scores from their best employees, using this data as a benchmark, to determine what traits are most beneficial in new candidates.

Physical

Physical examinations are used to ascertain if candidates are able to carry out the physical demands and duties of a job. Due to discrimination laws, employers cannot make you take a physical until after a job offer has been made.

Step 6: (The Interview)

When your marketing efforts start to payoff, you'll begin getting interviews. To be completely prepared, you'll want to look back at Chapter 5 under Formal Communication in the section titled Pre-Employment and in the section titled Selling-Closing the Deal further ahead in this chapter.

Step 7: (Negotiation)

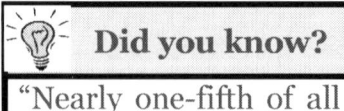

> **Did you know?**
> "Nearly one-fifth of all employees NEVER negotiate their salary when they accept a job"
> www.salary.com

Negotiation, per Wikipedia, is defined in part as "a dialogue between two or more people or parties, intended to reach an understanding, resolve a point of difference, or gain advantage in outcome." In other words, it's a give and take process in order to reach some compromise. When you agree to a job offer from an employer, a compromise has been reached regarding what you will be paid. Depending upon your negotiating skills, this can have a profound effect on how much you can earn over your lifetime.

Negotiating, like selling, is rarely included in our formal education system and is often learned through the school of hard knocks. Before you find yourself at the negotiating table, consider the following:

The Complete Picture

Before accepting a job, make sure you understand the total benefits package offered by the employer. Your salary (fixed amount per pay period) or hourly rate will likely be just one component of the benefits you will receive. Other employer-provided benefits often include health, dental, and eye insurance, paid vacation, sick leave, personal days, and retirement plans to name just a few. These extra benefits can make up as much as 30% of the total employer-provided benefits package. Therefore, do your homework and figure out what all these benefits are worth. This becomes especially important when comparing job offers from different companies.

Comparing benefits offered by two or more companies is a good problem to have and shows your job hunting efforts are working. Salary.com makes this job easier with its benefits wizard and can be found at:

http://swz.salary.com/MyBenefits/LayoutScripts/Mbfl_Start.aspx

Use this tool to find the average costs of benefits provided by an employer for a particular industry (healthcare, construction, transportation, education, etc.). Calculate, compare, and decide before making a decision.

Know the salary range

This was discussed previously as part of the four P's of marketing, and specifically addressed in the section on Price. Before going on an interview, try and find out the salary range of the position. Knowing this will allow you to negotiate toward the higher end of the range.

The offer

Is there any room to negotiate? Prior research will help you determine if the employer's offer is within your acceptable range.

The counter-offer

What if you feel the offer is too low? Your counter-offer must include a valid reason why you should be paid more. Make sure it is well thought out by showing how your past accomplishments will help the employer reach departmental and/or company goals.

Bargaining power (leverage)

Your effectiveness at salary negotiations is tied to your current employment status. Being employed while interviewing for a similar or higher paying job is ideal and gives you a distinct advantage in the bargaining process. Prospective employers know candidates currently employed have more leverage in this process and are less likely to leave their present position, unless the new position is more compelling (higher salary, better benefits and working conditions, etc.). If you currently have a job, use this power to negotiate toward the higher end of the salary range.

If you aren't employed or it's your first real job, you may have to accept the employer's offer. To make up for your temporarily weak bargaining position, ask for a review in three to six months to revisit this issue. Employers that are willing to negotiate, see value in you and what you have to offer the company. Know your value, and don't be afraid to articulate it during the negotiating process.

Selling - Closing the Deal

Successful businesses get their products or services in front of people most likely to buy them. These buyers (decision-makers) have the ability, power, and resources to make the purchase. Your goal needs to be the same. Get in front of the people (interviewers) who have the power and authority to hire you. A large portion of this book is devoted to helping you do just that through the use of effective marketing techniques.

If you have read this book, taken our advice, and done your homework, your marketing efforts will begin presenting you with selling opportunities. Marketing and selling have a cause and effect relationship and can be summed up by an old business adage, "Marketing is everything you do to make the phone ring. Selling is what you do when you pick up the phone." Will you be ready when the phone rings?

Many people cringe at the mere thought of having to sell something to someone else. Yet, if you want to reach your goals and reach your full potential, you'll have to sell the merits of your skills and abilities many times throughout your career. As noted previously, the Bureau of Labor Statistics says that, **"The median number of years that wage and salary workers had been with their current employer was 4.4 in January 2010."** If the average career lasts approximately 40 years, that means you may end up working for 9 or 10 different employers. The good news, this translates into opportunities (interviews, performance reviews, etc.) in which you have the chance to significantly increase your paycheck. Even receiving small increases, of say 10% a few times in your career, can have a big impact on how much you earn over your working lifetime.

Figure 6.9 below illustrates this difference by showing a side by side comparison of two employees and their salary history over a forty year period. In year 1, they each make $25,000 and receive pay increases of three percent per year thereafter. Employee B however, receives a ten percent pay increase in years 10, 20, and 30 instead of three percent. While this difference may appear small at the time, it has big ramifications when we look at the career earnings for both employees. This seemingly small difference results in employee B making over $250,000 more than Employee A over a forty-year career.

Figure 6.9 – Career Earnings Example

Year	Employee A	Employee B
1	25,000	25,000
2	25,750	25,750
3	26,523	26,523
4	27,318	27,318
5	28,138	28,138
6	28,982	28,982
7	29,851	29,851
8	30,747	30,747
9	31,669	31,669
10	32,619	34,836
11	33,598	35,881
13	34,606	36,958
14	35,644	38,066
15	36,713	39,208
16	37,815	40,385
17	38,949	41,596
18	40,118	42,844
19	41,321	44,129
20	42,561	48,542
21	43,838	49,999
22	45,153	51,499
23	46,507	53,044
24	47,903	54,635
25	49,340	56,274
26	50,820	57,962
27	52,344	59,701
28	53,915	61,492
29	55,532	63,337
30	57,198	69,670
31	58,914	71,761
32	60,682	73,913
33	62,502	76,131
34	64,377	78,415
35	66,308	80,767
36	68,298	83,190
37	70,347	85,686
38	72,457	88,256
39	74,631	90,904
40	76,870	93,631
Totals	$1,805,856	$2,056,691

Therefore, it's very important to recognize the opportunities (new job, promotion, contract renewal, etc.) placed before you and to act on them. To earn what you deserve, you must believe in yourself, and be able to effectively communicate your demands at the appropriate time.

Using the analogy above, what will you do when you pick up the phone? In other words, how will you sell "you?" Will you close the deal and get the job, promotion, or bonus you deserve? Below are some suggestions to help you become a better salesperson when the opportunity presents itself. Some of this has previously been discussed in Chapter 5 (Communication) but the following five items are worth repeating due to their importance.

Use Your Resources

Use everything available to show your value. This pre-sales preparation should be done prior to your interview, performance review, promotional opportunities, etc.

- ➢ *Resume* - Make sure it is rock solid by using our tips and techniques from Chapter 1. If you have modified it to take in the job description, you should know it inside and out and be ready to respond to the interviewer's questions.

- ➢ *Portfolio* - Sales are about setting yourself apart from the competition. Nothing does that better than showing the interviewer tangible evidence of your accomplishments. This immediately elevates your status and puts you into the serious contender category. Heed the advice in Chapter 2 and construct a portfolio. Odds are, most of the other candidates will not take the time to make one.

Do your homework

Great salespeople prepare and then prepare some more. They know their product better than anyone else and know their customers better than anyone else.

- ➢ *Best qualities* - Prior to the interview, take time to list your best qualities. Employers look for these in the questions they ask either directly or subtly. Be prepared to say them directly if asked or use them in the context of your experiences. What kinds of qualities are employers looking for in a candidate? Someone who is positive, mature, flexible, open to new ideas, and takes into consideration the welfare of others to name just a few. In essence, they are looking for those candidates who have the best attitude.

➤ *Be the solution* - Companies hire people to solve problems. Are you the solution? You can be if you know what the problem is. How does the advertised position relate to the overall mission of the business? It's up to you to find out by doing your homework. Do your research and find out as much as possible about the company and the position you are interviewing for. You can do this by:

- ❖ Checking out the company website.
- ❖ Searching the company's name on the Internet.
- ❖ Asking around for information. Know an insider (someone who works there)?

If you have the right answers, you'll likely get the job.

Control the Dialogue

➤ *Listen* - This seems counterintuitive. How can I control the dialogue if I am not talking? The best sales people listen more than they speak. It allows them to learn about their customers and the types of problems they are having. Once the problem is known, a specific solution can be crafted or recommended. Listening will give you clues about the job, the company, and the type of person they need and allow you to ask pointed and relevant questions.

➤ *Ask Questions* - The interview should not be a one-way bombardment of questions. If it is, you're unlikely to get the job because you won't have enough time building a case as to why you are the best candidate. It should be a dialogue between two or more people, trying to get to know each other, to see if it is a good fit for both parties. The most productive interviews create an environment that allows all the participants to speak in an open and honest way.

- *Silence* - Don't make mindless chatter to fill in the gaps of silence during the interview. It will make you appear nervous and too anxious to please the interviewer. It is okay to pause and appear thoughtful before answering a question.

Close the deal

- *Be specific* - Cite examples of how your past work positively affected the company. Did it save time, money, resources, all of the above? Prepare sound bytes that tell how you did it. An example may be how you were part of a reorganizing team that streamlined operations and resulted in cost savings of $22,000 last year. Examples like this should be listed on your resume and are discussed more in-depth in Chapter 1. Only list and mention items you worked on and have intimate knowledge about. Otherwise, you may not be able to answer detailed questions regarding your experiences. Know yourself and don't stretch the truth.

- *Potential* - More than anything, employers want to make sure candidates will be a good fit with their organization. To get the most accurate picture possible, they employ a variety of methods (screenings, tests, interviews, etc.). Ultimately, they have to make a judgment call and take a chance. Your job is to make the employer feel comfortable by lessening the perceived risk in hiring you. How do you do that? Tie your past behavior and current skill sets to the future needs of the employer.

- *Ask* - This is a required step in the process many salespeople fail to take. They do all the right things during their sales presentation but don't ask for the sale. While you may not ask directly for the job in the first interview, you should ask questions that move the discussions in that direction. Some possible things to ask are:

    - What is the next step?
    - When do you think you will make a decision?
    - Do you feel I am one of the leading candidates?

    You have to ask to make the sale. Don't be afraid to do so.

Follow-up

This is the last step in the sales cycle and was previously discussed in Chapter 5. Because it is so important, we want to reiterate the value of this seemingly small act. Good salespeople make sure to follow-up with their customers on a regular and consistent basis. It allows them to show their gratitude, make sure the customer is satisfied with their purchase, and to take care of any issues or complaints in a timely manner.

You must also incorporate follow-up into your routine. Communicating with the interviewer after the interview shows proper etiquette, interest in the position, and the ability to follow-through. It also has consequences. From a national survey done by CareerBuilder, more than one-in-five (22%) of hiring managers say they are less likely to hire a candidate if they don't send a thank-you note after an interview. They also noted, a thank you note doesn't necessarily have to be handwritten; the majority (89%) of hiring managers says it's OK to send a thank-you note in the form of an email, with half saying it is actually the way they prefer to receive them.

Don't be discouraged or intimidated. It can take time and plenty of practice before you feel comfortable enough to try the tactics we mention above. However, the sooner you begin, the sooner you'll be paid what you deserve.

The Wrap-up

While this may be the end of the book, it's just the beginning for you. If you have taken our suggestions you now know:

- How to write resumes and cover letters that get you noticed, get you interviews, and best of all get you the jobs you want. (Chapters 1 & 5)
- The importance of documenting your experiences and how to present them in a way that showcases your value and forecasts your potential. (Chapter 2)
- How to research and choose the right educational resources that align with your personal and professional needs. (Chapter 3)
- The basic financial fundamentals that affect every aspect of your life. (Chapter 4)
- Why communication is so important in every interaction. (Chapter 5)
- How to market yourself in a way that reveals your true value while getting compensated accordingly. (Chapter 6)

Use this information to get better at:

- Communicating (writing, speaking, and interacting with others).
- Knowing and utilizing the resources around you.
- Making better financial decisions.
- Increasing your worth by utilizing the proper promotional methods.

Finally, we'll leave you with a timeless quote from Mark Twain who said, "The secret of getting ahead is getting started. The secret of getting started is breaking your complex overwhelming tasks into small manageable tasks, and then starting on the first one."

About the Author

Donald Reinsel is an entrepreneur, educator, and writer who straddles all three disciplines in his quest to help individuals and businesses reach their true potential. For more information about the author and the Career Puzzle, go to www.thecareerpuzzle.com.

Index

A

accomplishments · 6, 12, 14, 16, 25, 26, 36, 37, 38, 39, 41, 56, 64, 66, 67, 135, 137, 150, 160, 187, 193, 211, 224, 230, 233
achievements · 10, 12, 14, 36, 38, 57, 67, 176, 210
activities · 25, 33, 34, 35, 58, 143
appearance · 8, 190
application · 5, 6, 9, 31, 60, 92, 136, 145, 205, 212, 219, 221, 222, 223, 225, 227
artifacts · 37, 38, 39, 42, 43, 45, 46, 47, 48, 51, 52, 57, 58, 59, 60, 61, 64, 66, 67, 187
awards · 3, 6, 55, 57, 177

B

background · 94, 224, 225
backups · 3
behavioral questions · 153, 154
binders · 45, 51
budget · 24, 25, 35, 92, 106, 107, 108, 111, 112, 113, 114, 115, 116, 117, 118, 119, 120, 122, 123, 124, 125, 126, 127, 128, 130, 177, 202

C

career fairs · 213
career services · 75, 78, 199
certifications · 6, 23, 57, 70, 77, 88, 217
contact information · 11, 12, 22, 23, 28, 66, 152, 165, 166, 203, 215
cover letter · 9, 10, 11, 22, 53, 135, 136, 137, 141, 146, 204, 218, 219, 220, 221, 225, 228
cover page · 51
credit cards · 92, 93, 99, 127, 129
credit checks · 94, 99, 226
credit rating · 93, 94, 95, 96, 97
credit report · 94, 95, 98, 100, 225, 226
credit reporting agencies · 93
credit reporting bureaus · 99
criminal background checks · 225

D

debit cards · 127
debt · 79, 80, 81, 92, 93, 99, 123, 129, 130, 131, 225
diet · 190, 193
duties · 9, 10, 12, 13, 14, 19, 21, 34, 86, 142, 143, 150, 163, 180, 181, 228

E

elevator pitch · 208
elevator speech · 23, 208, 209, 212, 214
email address · 11, 56, 66, 222, 223
executive Profile · 23, 35

F

financing · 93, 94, 95
fitness · 190, 196, 227
flash drive · 4, 5, 42, 45, 65
font size · 12
formal communication · 134, 183
formal learning · 70

G

google docs · 5, 31, 128, 166, 203
grade point average · 16, *See* GPA

H

heading · 12, 14, 16, 20
honesty · 94, 227
honors · 3, 55

I

informal communication · 133, 183
informal learning · 70
interview attire · 191
Introduction Letter · 52, 53, 54, 55, 60

J

job boards · 187, 216
job duties · 9

L

letter of introduction · 39
letters of recommendation · 39, 52, 53, 56

M

marketing · 8, 145, 187, 188, 189, 205, 215, 230
microsoft Word · 2, 5, 26, 44, 55, 59

N

negotiations · 158, 163, 181, 199, 230
networking · 75, 206, 208, 212, 214, 216

O

objective · 22, 23, 33, 34, 143

P

page protectors · 45, 47, 51

paper · 5, 47, 128, 136
personal development · 58
personal finance · 8, 92
phones · 118, 119
portfolio · 7, 37, 43, 49, 64, 66, 69, 191, 192, 193, 233
presentations · 169, 170
proofread · 7, 30

R

references · 28, 29, 39, 52, 53, 56, 60, 222, 223

S

salary range · 174, 197, 229, 230
sales pipeline · 8, 6, 145, 217, 218
salutation · 138
selling · 8, 145, 187, 188, 199, 228, 230
situational questions · 155
social media · 31, 82, 85, 150, 167, 169, 171, 181, 182, 206
summary of qualifications · 23, 25

T

the cloud · 4, 5
transcripts · 39, 57

W

white space · 9
work experience · 12, 19, 21, 34, 35, 52, 53, 58, 143, 210

Made in the USA
Charleston, SC
11 June 2015